pocket posh christmas
logic

100 PUZZLES

Andrews McMeel
Publishing, LLC

Kansas City · Sydney · London

POCKET POSH® CHRISTMAS LOGIC

10 11 12 13 14 LEO 10 9 8 7 6 5 4 3 2 1

ISBN: 978-0-7407-9960-0

Puzzles supplied under license from Arcturus Publishing.

Illustration by Kate Spain

www.andrewsmcmeel.com
www.puzzlesociety.com

ATTENTION: SCHOOLS AND BUSINESSES
Andrews McMeel books are available at quantity discounts
with bulk purchase for educational, business, or sales
promotional use. For information, please write to: Special
Sales Department, Andrews McMeel Publishing, LLC,
1130 Walnut Street, Kansas City, Missouri 64106.

how to solve a logic puzzle

Never tried a logic puzzle before? Don't worry! It's really not that hard. All you need is patience and a methodical approach to sort out the positive (yes) and negative (no) information you are given. All the relevant facts are there on the page in front of you.

Let's take things step by step. To make identification easier for beginners, we've lettered the squares of the grid in this example.

	Surname			Hair		
	Dale	Hill	Lake	Black	Brown	Red
Amy	A	B	C	D	E	F
Bill	G	H	I	J	K	L
Colin	M	N	O	P	Q	R
Black	S	T	U			
Brown	V	W	X			
Red	Y	Z	Ω			

Three children each have different surnames and different hair colors. Which is which?

1. The redhead surnamed Dale isn't Bill.

2. Colin (whose hair is brown) isn't the child surnamed Lake.

Child	Surname	Hair

Now start filling in the grid, using ✗s for the "no" (negative) and ✓s for the "yes" (positive) information given in the clues.

Clue 1 states that the redhead is surnamed Dale, so put a ✓ in square Y and ✗s in squares S, V, Z, and Ω. Clue 1 also states that Bill isn't the redhead, so put an ✗ in square L. Thus since Bill isn't surnamed Dale, put an ✗ in square G. Your grid now looks like this:

	Surname			Hair		
	Dale	Hill	Lake	Black	Brown	Red
Amy						
Bill	✗					✗
Colin						
Black	✗					
Brown	✗					
Red	✓	✗	✗			

Clue 2 states that Colin has brown hair, so put a ✓ in square Q and **X**s in squares P, R, E, and K. Your grid now looks like this:

	Surname			Hair		
	Dale	Hill	Lake	Black	Brown	Red
Amy					X	
Bill	X				X	X
Colin				X	✓	X
Black	X					
Brown	X					
Red	✓	X	X			

Since there are **X**s in both squares K and L, the only possibility remaining for Bill's hair color is black; so you can put a ✓ into square J and an **X** in square D.

The child with red hair is thus Amy, so put a ✓ in square F. Since the red-haired child is surnamed Dale (clue 1), you can put a ✓ in square A and **X**s in squares B, C, and M.

The child surnamed Lake isn't Colin (clue 2), so Bill; thus you can put a ✓ in square I and **X**s in squares H and O. Since Colin has brown hair, you can put an **X** in square X and thus a ✓ in W. The child surnamed Hill is thus Colin, so put a ✓ in square N.

Now you can fill the solution box with the details.

Your finished grid and solution box now look like this:

	Surname			Hair		
	Dale	Hill	Lake	Black	Brown	Red
Amy	✓	X	X	X	X	✓
Bill	X	X	✓	✓	X	X
Colin	X	✓	X	X	✓	X
Black	X	X	✓			
Brown	X	✓	X			
Red	✓	X	X			

Child	Surname	Hair
Amy	Dale	Red
Bill	Lake	Black
Colin	Hill	Brown

pocket posh® christmas logic

100 PUZZLES

Wild West Round-ups

In the 1880s, four sheriffs in neighboring towns decided to put an end to the gun-toting gangs that were terrorizing their communities. They gathered together posses of men and each tracked down and captured their quarry. To which isolated ranch did each sheriff track a gang, how many men were in his posse, and in which year did the capture take place?

1. The sheriff who led his men to Pedro's did so three years after a posse of 29 men led by Mitch Murphy had made their capture.

2. There were more members of the posse that surrounded the Golden Oak Ranch in 1887 than in the group led by Bill Barnes, who made his capture two years before Eddie Hill.

3. Sam Peters and his posse of 38 men did not visit the Lazy K Ranch.

	Golden Oak	Lazy K	Pedro's	Silver Steer	29	33	38	42	1882	1884	1885	1887
Bill Barnes												
Eddie Hill												
Mitch Murphy												
Sam Peters												
1882												
1884												
1885												
1887												
29 men												
33 men												
38 men												
42 men												

Sheriff	Ranch	Posse	Year

Playing Cards

The four men in this puzzle are playing a game of cards and each has three in his hand: one club, one diamond, and one spade. Can you discover which three cards each man holds? (NB: A=ace, J=jack, Q=queen, and K=king; and in the game, ace=1, jack=11, queen=12, king=13, and the values of the other cards are as per their numbers.)

1. Jeff's club has a value one higher than that of Paul's spade.

2. The man with the four of clubs has a diamond with a value two higher than that of the spade held by Raymond (who hasn't the four of clubs).

3. The man with the king of diamonds has a spade with a value three higher than that of the diamond held by Paul.

4. Norman's diamond has a lower value than that of his club.

		Club				Diamond				Spade			
		3	4	10	J	4	7	Q	K	A	2	7	10
	Jeff												
	Norman												
	Paul												
	Raymond												
Spade	A												
	2												
	7												
	10												
Diamond	4												
	7												
	Q												
	K												

Player	Club	Diamond	Spade

Dinner Discussions

Four friends meet up once a week for dinner, with each providing a meal in turn. On which date last month did every person hold his or her dinner party, at what time did it start, and what was the main topic of conversation?

	Date				Time				Topic			
	6th	13th	20th	27th	7:00 P.M.	7:15 P.M.	7:45 P.M.	8:00 P.M.	Education	Health	Politics	Religion
Charles												
Helen												
Margaret												
Patrick												
Education												
Health												
Politics												
Religion												
7:00 P.M.												
7:15 P.M.												
7:45 P.M.												
8:00 P.M.												

1. Margaret's dinner party started a quarter of an hour later than the one at which politics was discussed.

2. Helen's dinner party started three quarters of an hour later than the one that took place on the 27th.

3. Charles held his dinner party two weeks before the one that started at 7:15 P.M.

4. Education was discussed at the dinner party held on the 6th, which started half an hour later than the one at which the friends discussed religion.

5. Health was the subject of the conversation held on the 20th.

Friend	Date	Time	Topic

Music to Their Ears

Four friends each play a different musical instrument and like to listen to the work of a different composer (not necessarily one who wrote music associated with the instrument he or she plays). Discover each friend's full name, the instrument he or she plays, and the preferred composer of each, by using the notes below.

	Surname				Instrument				Composer			
	Border	Jacobs	Moore	Wilson	Oboe	Piano	Tuba	Violin	Brahms	Handel	Mahler	Mozart
Dawn												
Martin												
Penny												
Stephen												
Brahms												
Handel												
Mahler												
Mozart												
Oboe												
Piano												
Tuba												
Violin												

1. Of the two women: one is engaged to be married to the man who likes to listen to Mahler; and the other is the pianist, whose surname isn't Jacobs.

2. Of the two men: one has the surname Border; and the other plays the oboe and prefers to listen to the music of Handel.

3. Of the person surnamed Moore and the tuba player: one prefers the music of Mahler; and the other is Penny.

4. Of the violin player and Stephen: one has the surname Wilson; and the other likes to listen to Brahms.

Friend	Surname	Instrument	Composer

Split Personalities

Naughty Nora has cut photographs of five of her relatives each into three pieces (head, body, and legs) and then reassembled them in such a way that each "new" picture contains pieces of three "old" ones. How have the pictures been reassembled?

1. Nora's grandpa's body is now attached to her cousin's legs, but her grandpa's head is in a different picture to that containing her cousin's body.

2. Nora's sister's body is now attached to her uncle's head, but her sister's legs aren't in the same picture as her uncle's body.

3. Nora's uncle's legs are in the same picture as her cousin's head.

		Body					Legs				
		Aunt	Cousin	Grandpa	Sister	Uncle	Aunt	Cousin	Grandpa	Sister	Uncle
Head	Aunt										
	Cousin										
	Grandpa										
	Sister										
	Uncle										
Legs	Aunt										
	Cousin										
	Grandpa										
	Sister										
	Uncle										

Head	Body	Legs

Hairdressing

Harriet offers a hairdressing service and visits women in their homes in order to style their hair. Yesterday she had five appointments; can you discover the time of each client's appointment, together with the color of her hair?

1. Harriet's appointment with the woman who has silver hair was in the morning, and her appointment with Jackie was in the afternoon (although it wasn't the last appointment of the day).

2. Harriet styled Kate's hair one hour later than the appointment with the blonde-haired client.

3. Harriet's appointment with the chestnut-haired woman (who isn't Iona) took place four hours earlier than her appointment with Molly, who has brown hair.

	10:00 A.M.	11:00 A.M.	2:00 P.M.	3:00 P.M.	4:00 P.M.	Black	Blonde	Brown	Chestnut	Silver
Iona										
Jackie										
Kate										
Louisa										
Molly										
Black										
Blonde										
Brown										
Chestnut										
Silver										

Client	Time	Hair

Refreshment

It's Judy's turn to get the afternoon refreshments in the office today. She's having tea and cookies, but (as is usual in a logic puzzle!) everyone else wants something different to drink with the choice of various donuts. Can you discover each person's order?

1. The person who wants a mug of hot cocoa also wants a plain donut (one with no topping or filling).

2. Mike wants coffee but not an iced donut.

3. Sandie wants a cherry-filled donut. Neither she nor the person who has asked for a cream donut ever drinks cola.

4. The person who wants a cream donut doesn't want coffee or juice to drink.

5. Tony doesn't want an iced donut and neither he nor Doris wants cocoa to drink.

	Drink					Donut				
	Cocoa	Coffee	Cola	Juice	Water	Cherry	Chocolate	Cream	Iced	Plain
Doris										
Mike										
Sandie										
Tony										
Will										
Cherry										
Chocolate										
Cream										
Iced										
Plain										

Name	Drink	Donut

Piece of Cake?

Caroline has baked a cake, which has a topping of walnuts and cherries. She and four friends are now going to eat it. The cherries are represented by black circles and the walnuts by white circles in the picture of the cake below. What is the full name of the person about to receive each slice?

1. Caroline's slice has one fewer cherry than on the slice to be given to the person surnamed Stone (who isn't Jonathan).

2. Kimberly Weaver's slice is next to and between that to be given to Jessica and the slice (not C) for the person surnamed Bourne.

3. George Crawford's slice has two walnuts, as has that which will be eaten by the person (not Jonathan) whose surname is Leigh.

	Caroline	George	Jessica	Jonathan	Kimberly	Bourne	Crawford	Leigh	Stone	Weaver
Slice A										
Slice B										
Slice C										
Slice D										
Slice E										
Bourne										
Crawford										
Leigh										
Stone										
Weaver										

Slice	Name	Surname

Octogenarians

The four couples who appear in this puzzle are all in their eighties. Can you discover who is married to whom and their respective ages?

1. Amy's husband is two years younger than Wendy. Wendy is younger than Graham.

2. David is younger than Eddie, but older than Tina's husband.

3. Eddie is either four years older or four years younger than Graham's wife.

4. Graham's wife is older than Frank's wife.

	Wife				His Age				Her Age			
	Amy	Barbara	Tina	Wendy	83	85	86	89	81	82	85	87
David												
Eddie												
Frank												
Graham												
Her Age 81												
Her Age 82												
Her Age 85												
Her Age 87												
His Age 83												
His Age 85												
His Age 86												
His Age 89												

Husband	Wife	His Age	Her Age

Every One a Winner

Five gamblers all bet on horses in different races yesterday afternoon and all won a small amount. What was the name of the horse on which each staked a bet and how much did he or she win?

1. Gordon won five dollars less than Frank, who won either twice as much or half as much as the gambler who placed a bet on Cry Wolf.

2. Escapade won $45 for one lucky gambler.

3. Whoever placed a bet on Albatross won twenty dollars more than Maggie.

4. Diane (who won more than the person who staked a bet on Braveheart) won either ten dollars more or ten dollars less than the backer of Dick's Choice.

	Albatross	Braveheart	Cry Wolf	Dick's Choice	Escapade	$20	$25	$40	$45	$50
Diane										
Frank										
Gordon										
Maggie										
Stan										
$20					
$25					
$40					
$45					
$50					

Gambler	Horse	Won

A Moving Story

Five couples are moving today. None is moving within the same state, so can you move through the clues to find where each is relocating from and to?

1. Mr. and Mrs. Evans are moving from Iowa. Mr. and Mrs. Black are moving from the state to which Mr. and Mrs. Evans are moving.

2. The state Mr. and Mrs. Fisher are leaving is the one to which Mr. and Mrs. Black are moving.

3. The couple relocating to Florida from California aren't Mr. and Mrs. Black or Mr. and Mrs. Drake.

4. Mr. and Mrs. Cooper are moving to Texas.

	From					To				
	California	Florida	Iowa	Ohio	Texas	California	Florida	Iowa	Ohio	Texas
Mr. and Mrs. Black										
Mr. and Mrs. Cooper										
Mr. and Mrs. Drake										
Mr. and Mrs. Evans										
Mr. and Mrs. Fisher										
California										
Florida										
Iowa										
Ohio										
Texas										

To

Couple	From	To

Patchwork Quilt

Molly has just started to make a patchwork quilt, sewing a different piece every day. Each is of a different color and has a different fruit stitched onto it. For each patch, can you work out the color and fruit, and decide the day on which it was made? NB: The terms left, right, higher, and lower are from your point of view as you look at the diagram below.

1. The green patch is farther left than the one made on Saturday.

2. The patch with the picture of a plum sewn onto it was made two days before the purple patch, which was made earlier in the week than the white patch.

3. The turquoise patch is higher than that with the picture of a cherry, which was made earlier in the week than the turquoise patch.

4. Patch C was made later in the week than the one with the picture of an apricot.

	Color				Fruit				Day			
	Green	Purple	Turquoise	White	Apricot	Cherry	Plum	Strawberry	Monday	Wednesday	Friday	Saturday
Patch A												
Patch B												
Patch C												
Patch D												
Monday												
Wednesday												
Friday												
Saturday												
Apricot												
Cherry												
Plum												
Strawberry												

Patch A	Patch B
Patch C	Patch D

Patch	Color	Fruit	Day

Lots of Work

Four administrators worked hard today, typing e-mails, letters, and memos. Can you discover the exact number of each type of correspondence every person produced?

1. Evelyn produced as many memos as the number of letters typed by Gloria and as many e-mails as the number of letters typed by Justin.

2. Terry typed more memos than e-mails.

3. Gloria typed one more e-mail than Justin.

4. Whoever typed 20 e-mails produced more memos than Gloria and two more letters than Terry.

	E-mails				Letters				Memos			
	17	18	20	21	16	17	18	19	15	16	17	19
Evelyn												
Gloria												
Justin												
Terry												
Memos 15												
16												
17												
19												
Letters 16												
17												
18												
19												

Name	E-mails	Letters	Memos

Socks Change

There was a power outage this morning, so five siblings dressed in the dark. It wasn't until they got onto the school bus that they realized they were each wearing one of their own socks and one belonging to another sister or brother. Coincidentally, each child had his or her own socks on the left foot and someone else's on the right. Can you discover the facts?

1. Lenny wore a blue sock on his right foot; it doesn't belong to Jenny.

2. One of the children wore a gray sock on the left foot and a white sock on the right foot.

3. Benny's socks are black; he wasn't wearing a gray sock on his right foot.

4. Kenny found that someone else was wearing one of his brown socks.

5. The child with a gray sock on the right foot wasn't wearing a blue sock on the left foot.

	Left (own)					Right (another's)				
	Black	Blue	Brown	Gray	White	Black	Blue	Brown	Gray	White
Benny										
Jenny										
Kenny										
Lenny										
Penny										
Right Black										
Blue										
Brown										
Gray										
White										

Child	Left	Right

Partygoer

Pauline has been invited to five parties, all to be held next month. Can you link each host to the reason he is holding his party and the date on which it will take place?

1. The party (not being hosted by Damian) to celebrate the graduation of one of Pauline's friends will be held earlier in the month than John's party.

2. Damian is hosting the party that will take place two days later than the one celebrating the launch of a book.

3. The birthday party will be held earlier in the month than that being hosted by Lester.

4. Phil is hosting a party to wish all his friends good-bye, as he is emigrating to another country. Phil's party will take place later in the month than the party celebrating one man's retirement from work.

	Birthday	Book launch	Emigration	Graduation	Retirement	10th	12th	15th	18th	20th
Damian										
Hugh										
John										
Lester										
Phil										
10th										
12th										
15th										
18th										
20th										

Host	Reason	Date

Ask an Expert

Ask an Expert is a weekly TV show during which members of the audience are invited to question the panel on a matter concerning them. Can you identify this week's panel members as shown in the picture below by his or her first name, surname, and field of expertise?

1. Brenda is next to and left of the gardening expert, who is next to and left of the oldest panel member.

2. Harry is seated next to and between the finance expert and the person surnamed Moorcroft.

3. The panel member surnamed Lowe is next to and right of Viola, who isn't sitting next to Sean (whose field of expertise is cooking).

4. The law specialist isn't the panel member whose surname is Wallis.

	Name				Surname				Field			
	Brenda	Harry	Sean	Viola	Lowe	Moorcroft	Stevenson	Wallis	Cooking	Finance	Gardening	Law
Person A												
Person B												
Person C												
Person D													
Cooking													
Finance													
Gardening													
Law													
Lowe													
Moorcroft													
Stevenson													
Wallis													

LEFT ⇐   RIGHT ⇒

A   B   C   D

Person	Name	Surname	Field

Photographic Memories

On a shelf in her room, Pamela has four photographs of aunts and uncles, all sadly now deceased. Can you discover who is featured in each picture, together with the month and year it was taken?

	Subject				Month				Year			
	Aunt Eliza	Aunt Jane	Uncle David	Uncle Joseph	April	June	August	October	1997	1999	2001	2003
Photo A												
Photo B												
Photo C												
Photo D												
1997												
1999												
2001												
2003												
April												
June												
August												
October												

LEFT ⇐   RIGHT ⇒

A B C D

Photo	Subject	Month	Year

1. The picture of Uncle Joseph is somewhere between the one taken in June and the one taken in 2001 (which is farther right than the picture of Aunt Jane).

2. The picture of Uncle David is farther left than the one taken in 1999, which, in turn, is farther left than the picture taken in August.

3. The picture of Aunt Eliza is directly next to the one taken in April (which isn't of Aunt Jane).

4. Photo A was taken in an earlier year (and in an earlier month of the year) than photo D.

5. No photograph was taken in October 2003.

Animals in the Garden

Four of Farmer Fletcher's fields abut his yard. He needs to repair the fences, however, he has found that his animals love to push through and climb over them, to get to the tasty herbs and flowers! Today, no fewer than four different types of animal got into the yard. At what time did he find each type, how many were there, and what were they eating?

1. There were more chickens in the garden than cows, which were found (but not at eleven o'clock) an hour and a half after the chickens.

2. Farmer Fletcher found the marigolds being munched 90 minutes after he caught the pigs in the yard. The pigs weren't eating parsley.

3. Five of his animals were found gorging in the sage bushes at half past twelve.

4. The sheep got into the yard in the afternoon.

5. There weren't four animals eating Farmer Fletcher's nasturtiums.

		Time				Number				Eating			
		9:30 A.M.	11:00 A.M.	12:30 P.M.	2:00 P.M.	3	4	5	6	Marigolds	Nasturtiums	Parsley	Sage
	Chickens												
	Cows												
	Pigs												
	Sheep												
Eating	Marigolds												
	Nasturtiums												
	Parsley												
	Sage												
Number	3												
	4												
	5												
	6												

Animals	Time	Number	Eating

Split Personalities

Naughty Nora has cut photographs of five of her relatives each into three pieces (head, body, and legs) and then reassembled them in such a way that each "new" picture contains pieces of three "old" ones. How have the pictures been reassembled?

1. Nora's aunt's rather plump body is now attached to her sister's somewhat spindly legs. However, her aunt's legs are in a different picture than that of her sister's head.

2. Nora's uncle's legs are in the same picture as her cousin's head.

3. Nora's sister's body is now firmly attached to her grandpa's head.

4. Nora's grandpa's legs and her sister's head are in two different pictures.

5. Nora's uncle's body and her aunt's head are in two different pictures.

		Body					Legs				
		Aunt	Cousin	Grandpa	Sister	Uncle	Aunt	Cousin	Grandpa	Sister	Uncle
Head	Aunt										
	Cousin										
	Grandpa										
	Sister										
	Uncle										
Legs	Aunt										
	Cousin										
	Grandpa										
	Sister										
	Uncle										

Head	Body	Legs

Racing Grannies

Four grandmothers rose to the spirit of the local school sports day by entering the senior women's sprint race. Can you discover who ran in each of the lanes marked on the plan below, together with her finishing position and the color of her tracksuit?

1. The grandmother who wore a pale lilac tracksuit ran in the lane next to and between Edith's and that of the woman who came in second.

2. Charlotte's lane had a number one higher than that of the woman who won the race.

3. Doreen finished one place behind the woman in the turquoise tracksuit, who ran in a lane with a lower number than Doreen's.

4. Frances (who didn't finish third) ran in a lane with a higher number than that of the woman (not Edith) who wore the pink tracksuit.

	Granny				Finished				Tracksuit			
	Charlotte	Doreen	Edith	Frances	First	Second	Third	Fourth	Beige	Lilac	Pink	Turquoise
Lane 1												
Lane 2												
Lane 3												
Lane 4												
Beige												
Lilac												
Pink												
Turquoise												
First												
Second												
Third												
Fourth												

LANE		FINISH
4		
3		
2		
1		

Lane	Granny	Finished	Tracksuit

Nonagenarians

The four couples in this puzzle are all in their nineties. Can you work out who is married to whom and their respective ages?

1. Edgar's wife is one year younger than Clarice's husband (who is older than Edgar).

2. There is a difference of four years between the ages of Norman and his wife.

3. Maud is two years younger than her husband, who is three years younger than Frances.

4. Harold is married to Naomi.

	Wife				His Age				Her Age			
	Clarice	Frances	Maud	Naomi	93	94	97	98	91	93	96	99
Edgar												
Harold												
Norman												
Philip												
Her Age 91												
93												
96												
99												
His Age 93												
94												
97												
98												

Husband	Wife	His Age	Her Age

School Friends

Five children have recently started in a new school and are now friends. Can you discover the name of each one's previous school, as well as his or her favorite school subject?

1. Drama is the favorite subject of the former pupil of St. Luke's.

2. Hal has never shown any interest in music.

3. Olga's favorite subject is science, unlike that of the boy previously at Fortcliff School.

4. Until last month, Peter was a pupil at Woodford School. His favorite subject is neither music nor art.

5. Caroline's favorite subject is neither music nor drama. She is not the former pupil of High Hill School.

	School					Subject				
	Fortcliff	High Hill	Portwood	St. Luke's	Woodford	Art	Drama	English	Music	Science
Caroline										
Hal										
John										
Olga										
Peter										
Art										
Drama										
English										
Music										
Science										

Friend	School	Subject

Colorful Cocktails

Beryl has just landed a wonderful job, which she starts tomorrow, so she and five of her friends are celebrating at Colin's Cocktail Bar on Main Street. Beryl needs a clear head for the morning, so she's drinking pineapple juice, but the other five women have ordered the drinks you see lined up on the bar below, each with a strange name and even stranger color! Can you identify each drink?

1. The Bee's Sting is next to and left of the drink called Dynamighty; both are farther left than the clear blue cocktail.

2. The drink known as Eve's Folly has a lurid green color and is somewhere between the pink cocktail and the one called Abe's Antidote.

3. The Cornucopia is next to and right of the dark brown cocktail, but farther left than the turquoise-colored drink.

	Abe's Antidote	Bee's Sting	Cornucopia	Dynamighty	Eve's Folly	Blue	Brown	Green	Pink	Turquoise
Drink A										
Drink B										
Drink C										
Drink D										
Drink E										
Blue					
Brown					
Green					
Pink					
Turquoise					

LEFT ⇐   RIGHT ⇒

A   B   C   D   E

Drink	Cocktail	Color

Door Colors

Five people who live in the houses shown below have painted their front doors in various colors. Can you discover the name of the occupant at each address, together with the color of his or her door?

1. The house with the blue door is farther north than Jimmy's and farther east than the house with the green front door.

2. The house with the red door has a number two higher than that of the oldest house that, in turn, has a higher number than that of the house with the cream front door.

3. Deborah lives directly south of Martin, who lives farther east than the person whose front door is black.

4. Pam's house has neither a red nor a black front door.

	Bill	Deborah	Jimmy	Martin	Pam	Black	Blue	Cream	Green	Red
No. 1										
No. 2										
No. 3										
No. 4										
No. 5										
Black						
Blue						
Cream						
Green						
Red						

House No.	Occupant	Door

Delegates in Delaware

Varying numbers of delegates from different states descended on Delaware for their corporations' annual conferences last year. Each conference was given a different title, reflecting each corporation's aims, aspirations, and/or message. For each of these titles, can you work out the number of delegates who attended and their states of origin?

1. More delegates attended the "Broad Outlook" conference than the one held by the corporation based in the state of Illinois.

2. The name of the state from which the "Great Ideas" conference delegates came has fewer letters than both the names of the states from which delegates had arrived for the "Broad Outlook" and "New Horizons" conferences.

3. Eighteen more attended the "Clients Count" conference than were present at the conference held by the corporation based in Texas.

4. The "Clients Count" conference wasn't that of the corporation based in Kansas, which had nine fewer attendees than the number at the "New Horizons" conference.

5. There were more than three hundred attendees at the "Fast Forward" conference.

	Delegates					State				
	265	283	292	301	319	Florida	Illinois	Kansas	Ohio	Texas
Broad Outlook										
Clients Count										
Fast Forward										
Great Ideas										
New Horizons										
Florida										
Illinois										
Kansas										
Ohio										
Texas										

Conference	Delegates	State

Families

Each of the four families in this puzzle is made up of a husband, wife, son, and daughter, whose names begin with four different letters of the alphabet. Can you decide who is related to whom?

1. Alan's wife isn't Dawn, and Dawn's daughter isn't Leonie.

2. Chrissie's son is Liam, whose sister isn't Debbie.

	Wife				Son				Daughter			
	Anne	Chrissie	Dawn	Lily	Aidan	Colin	Damian	Liam	Angelica	Carolyn	Debbie	Leonie
Alan												
Charles												
Dicky												
Larry												
Angelica												
Carolyn												
Debbie												
Leonie												
Aidan												
Colin												
Damian												
Liam												

(Left labels: Daughter for Angelica/Carolyn/Debbie/Leonie; Son for Aidan/Colin/Damian/Liam)

Husband	Wife	Son	Daughter

The Puppet-Maker

Paulus Petronelli is a puppet-maker. Last December, he was sitting in his shop, when he looked up to see the noses of five small children pressed against his windowpane, each child eyeing a puppet he or she dearly hoped to get for Christmas! The wishes of the children were granted, of course, and each is now the proud owner of one of Paulus's unique creations. Can you link each child to the type of puppet he or she received, and the name by which it is known?

1. Arabella, the stately ballet dancer, is owned by one of the girls, while another of the girls owns the pixie puppet.

2. The dragon's name is (appropriately) Snort.

3. Katie has named her puppet Clacker. Her brother Dean owns the mule puppet.

4. Anne owns the clown puppet. She hasn't named him Walpole.

	Type					Puppet's Name				
	Ballet dancer	Clown	Dragon	Mule	Pixie	Arabella	Clacker	Mosie	Snort	Walpole
Anne										
Benjamin										
Dean										
Katie										
Louisa										
Arabella										
Clacker										
Mosie										
Snort										
Walpole										

Child	Type	Name

Busy Couriers

The five people listed below all work as motorbike couriers for a company based in New York. Yesterday was a very busy day, with each delivering a different number of parcels and traveling a different number of miles. Travel through the clues to discover the details.

1. The courier who traveled 96 miles delivered one more parcel than David.

2. The courier who traveled 92 miles delivered one more parcel than Carl.

3. The courier who delivered 16 parcels traveled six fewer miles than Sandra.

4. The courier who delivered 12 parcels traveled four fewer miles than Richard.

5. The courier who traveled 88 miles delivered two fewer parcels than Laura.

	Parcels					Miles				
	11	12	14	15	16	86	88	92	96	98
Carl										
David										
Laura										
Richard										
Sandra										
86 miles					
88 miles					
92 miles					
96 miles					
98 miles					

Courier	Parcels	Miles

Florida Fairs

Hal has always had an interest in collecting old things and regularly visits antique fairs in the hope of obtaining an item or two. Last year, he attended four in his native state of Florida, each in a different season. Can you discover the location of every fair, the subject of each, and the amount Hal spent there?

1. The fair held in Orlando was later in the year than the one at which Hal spent $120 more than he paid for books at the Tampa Antique Fair.

2. Hal didn't buy clothing at the Sarasota Summer Fair, at which he spent $240 more than he paid for some rather nice pieces of porcelain to add to his collection.

3. Hal spent the least amount of money in Miami, which he visited later in the year than the antique fair at which he bought clothing.

	Location				Subject				Spent			
	Miami	Orlando	Sarasota	Tampa	Books	Clothing	Paintings	Porcelain	$550	$670	$790	$910
Spring												
Summer												
Autumn												
Winter												
$550												
$670												
$790												
$910												
Books												
Clothing												
Paintings												
Porcelain												

Season	Location	Subject	Spent

Fortunate Folk

Four friends consulted a fortune-teller, who predicted various things for each, using different methods. What was the fortune-teller's prediction for every person, by what method was it foretold, and during what period of time will it happen?

1. The prediction of a career change came as a result of reading tea leaves, but wasn't given to Christopher, who is looking forward to something happening next month.

2. A crystal ball was used for the prediction of something about to happen next Tuesday.

3. Felicity is looking forward to a proposal of marriage, which will happen earlier than Mark's trip abroad, revealed as the result of a palm reading.

	Predicted				Method				Period			
	Career change	Inheritance	Marriage	Trip abroad	Crystal ball	Palm reading	Tarot cards	Tea leaves	Tomorrow	Next Tuesday	Next Friday	Next month
Christopher												
Felicity												
Mark												
Sharon												
Tomorrow													
Next Tuesday													
Next Friday													
Next month													
Crystal ball													
Palm reading													
Tarot cards													
Tea leaves													

Friend	Predicted	Method	Period

Charity Donations

While in the shopping mall this afternoon, the four people in this puzzle each bought a sticker from a volunteer who was selling them in aid of a charity. To which type of charity did each shopper make a donation, what was that donation, and who was the volunteer collector in each case?

	Animals	Birds	Children	War widows	$2	$3	$4	$5	Faith	Honor	Hope	Verity
Sadie												
Sally												
Shane												
Stan												
Faith												
Honor												
Hope												
Verity												
$2												
$3												
$4												
$5												

1. Shane supported the charity in aid of the protection of birds and their habitats.

2. Sally (who didn't donate to the charity for sick animals) bought her sticker from Faith.

3. One of the shoppers gave $5 to the charity for which Hope was collecting.

4. Sadie donated one dollar more (but not to Hope's charity) than the amount given to the children's charity by Stan.

5. Verity collected $4 from one of the shoppers.

Shopper	Charity	Donation	Collector

From Stage to Screen

Four actresses have recently moved from the theater to the world of television and each now hosts her own talk show. Can you discover every woman's full name, the title of the last stage play in which she starred, and the title of her television show?

1. The four women are: Cathy; Ms. Grant; the former star of *Stephanie*; and the woman (not Ms. Fisher) who hosts *Talk to Me*.

2. The four women are: Norma, Patsy (who isn't Ms. Fisher); the former star of *Old Habits*; and the woman who hosts *Good Evening*.

3. Three of the women are: the former star (not Ms. Donelly) of *Old Habits*; the one (not Norma) who hosts *Ask a Friend*; and the one who hosts *Why Not?*

	Donelly	Fisher	Grant	Jones	Cloud Nine	Joking Apart	Old Habits	Stephanie	Ask a Friend	Good Evening	Talk to Me	Why Not?
Surname												
Cathy												
Madeleine												
Norma												
Patsy												
Ask a Friend												
Good Evening												
Talk to Me												
Why Not?												
Cloud Nine												
Joking Apart												
Old Habits												
Stephanie												

4. Three of the women are: Ms. Fisher; the former star of *Cloud Nine*; and the former star (not Patsy) of *Joking Apart*.

Hostess	Surname	Last Play	TV Show

Jigsaw Puzzle

Five people are enjoying the jigsaw puzzles they have recently acquired. Can you name the person trying to recreate each picture and say how many pieces each puzzle comprises?

1. The jigsaw of the New York City skyline has twice as many pieces as Harold's puzzle, but not as many pieces as Juan's (which isn't of horses).

2. Deborah's puzzle has a scene of the Rocky Mountains. It has more pieces than the jigsaw of flowers, but fewer than both the jigsaw of horses and that of the harbor scene.

3. Kathleen's puzzle has more pieces than Peter's, although not twice as many.

	Deborah	Harold	Juan	Kathleen	Peter	750	1,000	1,500	2,000	3,000
City skyline										
Flowers										
Harbor										
Horses										
Mountains										
750 pieces										
1,000 pieces										
1,500 pieces										
2,000 pieces										
3,000 pieces										

Puzzle	Person	Pieces

New Teachers

Five new teachers joined the staff of Waterford Elementary School at the beginning of the year, all of whom had been employed in other jobs before entering the profession. Can you work through the clues to find out each person's previous line of employment and the subject he or she now teaches?

	Former Job					Teaches				
	Accountant	Bank clerk	Mechanic	Store manager	Tailor	Biology	Geography	History	Mathematics	Music
Miss Arran										
Mr. Cole										
Mrs. Doyle										
Ms. Foster										
Mr. Gold										
Biology										
Geography										
History										
Mathematics										
Music										

1. The former accountant who now teaches history is neither Mr. Cole nor Mrs. Doyle.

2. Miss Arran (who teaches neither mathematics nor music) was once employed as a bank clerk.

3. Ms. Foster, who now teaches geography, has never worked as a tailor or as a mechanic.

4. Mr. Cole is not a music teacher.

5. The former mechanic does not teach mathematics.

Name	Former Job	Teaches

Commuters

Four men who work for the same company travel to and from work by train each day, always occupying the same seats. The plan below shows those seats; the men in seats A and B have their backs to the engine and are facing those in seats C and D. Can you put the correct first name and surname to the occupant of each seat, as well as discover the department in which he works?

	First Name				Surname				Dept			
	David	Edward	Frank	George	Bourne	Collins	Davis	Edmonton	Finance	Marketing	Personnel	Sales
Seat A												
Seat B												
Seat C												
Seat D												
Finance												
Marketing												
Personnel												
Sales												
Bourne												
Collins												
Davis												
Edmonton												

Direction of Travel

```
 A  B

 C  D
```

1. David (who has his back to the engine) is seated directly opposite the person who works in the Finance Department, who sits next to the person surnamed Collins.

2. The employee surnamed Davis sits directly opposite the one who works in the Sales Department, who sits next to Frank.

3. Edward's seat faces the direction of travel and isn't directly opposite that occupied daily by the Marketing Department employee.

4. The occupant of seat D is surnamed Edmonton.

Seat	Name	Surname	Dept

Apples and Pears

The five people in this puzzle all enjoy eating fresh fruit. Last week, each stocked up on various quantities of apples and pears. Can you discover the amounts each purchased?

1. Ruth bought one more apple than Kenny but fewer pears than Barbara.

2. The person who bought one fewer apple than George also bought one more pear than Steve.

3. Steve bought two more apples than Barbara, who bought one fewer pear than George.

4. Kenny bought two more apples than pears.

	Apples					Pears				
	7	8	9	10	11	8	9	10	11	12
Barbara										
George										
Kenny										
Ruth										
Steve										
8										
9										
10										
11										
12										

Pears

Name	Apples	Pears

Dress Buys

The five women in this puzzle each bought two new dresses yesterday. Can you discover how much they paid for both their first and second purchases? No two women spent the same as any other for a dress, nor did any woman's second purchase cost the same as her first.

1. Beth's second purchase was $10 more than her first.

2. Carly's second purchase was $5 more than her first.

3. The woman who spent $60 on her first purchase spent more on her second than Fran's second purchase, but $15 less on her second than Donna's second purchase.

	First					Second				
	$40	$45	$50	$55	$60	$30	$40	$45	$55	$60
Beth										
Carly										
Donna										
Edina										
Fran										
$30					
$40					
$45					
$55					
$60					

(Second)

Name	First	Second

Cushions

Catherine enjoys making needlepoint cushions. The five you see on the sofa in the picture below were all made in different months last year. Can you discover when each was made, together with the picture on each one?

1. The cushion with a picture of a Siamese cat is next to and left of that depicting birds in flight, which was made four months after cushion D, which hasn't a picture of a cat or roses.

2. Cushion B (which hasn't a picture of birds) was made four months earlier than the cushion next to and left of that with a picture of sunflowers.

3. Cushion E was made in April.

	Month					Picture				
	February	April	June	August	October	Apple tree	Birds	Cat	Roses	Sunflowers
Cushion A										
Cushion B										
Cushion C										
Cushion D										
Cushion E										
Apple tree										
Birds										
Cat										
Roses										
Sunflowers										

LEFT ⇦   RIGHT ⇨

A B C D E

Cushion	Month	Picture

Grandchildren

Five of Doreen's granddaughters gave birth last week, so now she's a great-grandmother, too! What is the name of the baby born to each woman and on which day did he or she come into the world?

1. Bella was born two days later than Leslie's child, but earlier in the week than Ruth.

2. Lynne's daughter was born the day before Liz's first child.

3. Christine was born the day before Alan, but the day after Lucy's baby.

	Baby					Day				
	Alan	Bella	Christine	Perry	Ruth	Monday	Tuesday	Wednesday	Thursday	Friday
Laura										
Leslie										
Liz										
Lucy										
Lynne										
Monday					
Tuesday					
Wednesday					
Thursday					
Friday					

Mother	Baby	Day

Lola's Lamps

Over the course of five days last week, Lola purchased five new lamps for her home, each of a different color. The picture below shows them lined up for your inspection. Can you work out which lamp she bought on the five consecutive days?

1. Lamp A was bought earlier in the week than the beige lamp, but later in the week than the lamp next to and left of the beige lamp.

2. The pink lamp is directly next to the one Lola bought on Friday, which isn't yellow.

3. Lamp D was bought later in the week than the pink lamp which, in turn, was bought later in the week than the orange lamp.

4. Lola bought the blue lamp on Wednesday and lamp E on Thursday.

	Lamp					Color				
	A	B	C	D	E	Beige	Blue	Orange	Pink	Yellow
Tuesday										
Wednesday										
Thursday										
Friday										
Saturday										
Beige										
Blue										
Orange										
Pink										
Yellow										

LEFT ⇐   RIGHT ⇒

A B C D E

Day	Lamp	Color

Viewing Habits

Five friends who share an apartment each have a favorite program that he or she insists on watching every week. Which program does each friend watch and on which evening of the week?

1. Michelle never watches *Laughter Time*, which is broadcast every Tuesday evening.

2. Shirley's favorite program is *News Review*.

3. *Sports World* is broadcast the evening before *Natural World*, which James never fails to watch.

4. Jose's favorite program is shown on Saturday evenings.

	Program					Evenings				
	Laughter Time	Natural World	News Review	Sports World	World Events	Mondays	Tuesdays	Thursdays	Fridays	Saturdays
James										
Jose										
Michelle											
Shirley										
Timothy										
Mondays					
Tuesdays					
Thursdays					
Fridays					
Saturdays					

Friend	Program	Evenings

Fun at the Fair

When they visited the fun-fair yesterday, the five children in this puzzle all enjoyed themselves, and each had multiple turns on the ride he or she liked best. What was each child's favorite and how many times did he or she take the ride?

1. Carole took her favorite ride more times than the number of turns taken on the big dipper (not Freddie's favorite ride).

2. The child whose favorite ride is the pirate boat had two fewer turns than the child whose favorite is the roller coaster, who had fewer turns than Michael.

3. Louis's favorite is the bumper cars. He went on more than three times, but had fewer turns than Sally, whose favorite ride isn't the merry-go-round.

	Liked					Times				
	Big dipper	Bumper cars	Merry-go-round	Pirate boat	Roller coaster	3	4	5	6	7
Carole										
Freddie										
Louis										
Michael										
Sally										
3 times										
4 times										
5 times										
6 times										
7 times										

Rider	Liked	Times

Shopping Trip

On her recent trip into town, Lucy browsed in five shops. In every shop she saw a friend who was also browsing. In what order did Lucy visit the listed shops and who did she see there?

1. Lucy saw Donna in the shop she visited directly after the drugstore.

2. Virginia wasn't in the supermarket. The supermarket wasn't the last store Lucy visited.

3. The clothes store was visited directly before the shoe shop, which, in turn, was visited directly before the store where she saw Virginia.

4. Lucy saw Carol in the bookshop, but she didn't see Ann in the shoe shop.

	Order					Friend				
	First	Second	Third	Fourth	Fifth	Ann	Carol	Donna	Karen	Virginia
Bookshop										
Clothes store										
Drugstore										
Shoe shop										
Supermarket										
Ann					
Carol					
Donna					
Karen					
Virginia					

Shop	Order	Friend

Accumulated Wealth

Gemma is due to marry her fifth husband next month and has an engagement ring to show! However, being tired of diamonds, emeralds, rubies, and sapphires (and who wouldn't be, given the chance?) she chose a pearl this time around. Her previous husbands had each given her a ring, necklace, and bracelet containing solely diamonds, emeralds, rubies, and sapphires, but no two men had given her the same, and none had given the same gem in more than one item. Use the clues to discover the contents of Gemma's jewelry box.

	Bracelet				Necklace				Ring			
	Diamonds	Emeralds	Rubies	Sapphires	Diamonds	Emeralds	Rubies	Sapphires	Diamonds	Emeralds	Rubies	Sapphires
Hal												
Kurt												
Maurice												
Robert												
Ring — Diamonds												
Ring — Emeralds												
Ring — Rubies												
Ring — Sapphires												
Necklace — Diamonds												
Necklace — Emeralds												
Necklace — Rubies												
Necklace — Sapphires												

1. Hal (who never gave Gemma diamonds) gave her a ring containing the same stones as were in the bracelet given by Maurice and the necklace given by Robert.

2. The husband who presented Gemma with a ring of four rubies also gave her a necklace of emeralds, but not a sapphire bracelet.

3. The sapphire necklace was a gift from Kurt.

Husband	Bracelet	Necklace	Ring

Word Games

Five friends took the word "Playtime" and challenged each other to find one four-letter word and one five-letter word made from the letters in "Playtime." They all managed to do this and there were no duplications of any word. Can you discover the two words each person made?

1. One of the two women made the words "Empty" and "Mile."

2. George isn't the player who made both the words "Item" and "Plate."

3. Will's four-letter word starts with an earlier letter of the alphabet than Tim's four-letter word. However, Will's five-letter word starts with a later letter of the alphabet than Tim's five-letter word.

4. Sarah's five-letter word used all of the letters to be found in her four-letter word.

5. George only made one word starting with a vowel.

| | Four Letters | | | | | Five Letters | | | | |
	Emit	Item	Meat	Mile	Pale	Ample	Empty	Imply	Metal	Plate
Andrea										
George										
Sarah										
Tim										
Will										
Ample										
Empty										
Imply										
Metal										
Plate										

Friend	Four Letters	Five Letters

Housing Problem

Five married couples live in the houses shown on the map below. Use the clues in order to discover the names of the husband and wife living at each address.

1. Edgar and his wife live next to and south of Sue and her husband, who live directly west of Wendy and her husband.

2. Rose and her husband Henry live next to and south of Tanya and her husband.

3. Danny and his wife live directly west of Gordon and his wife.

	Wife					House No.				
	Rose	Sue	Tanya	Vera	Wendy	1	2	3	4	5
Danny										
Edgar										
Gordon										
Henry										
Ivan										
No. 1										
No. 2										
No. 3										
No. 4										
No. 5										

N
W E
S

```
 _____

 | 1 |    | 2 |

 | 3 |    | 4 |

 | 5 |
```

Husband	Wife	House No.

Happy Birthday

Four women each sent one birthday card last week to a friend who lives in a city abroad. When did each woman post her card, what is the name of her friend, and in which city does each friend live?

1. The card to Aileen was posted three days later than the one to Johannesburg.

2. Madge posted her card later in the week than the one to Rome, but earlier in the week than the one sent by Muriel to Amy, who doesn't live in Tokyo.

3. Aster's card was sent by Miriam, but not to an address in Rome.

	Day				Friend				City			
	Monday	Tuesday	Thursday	Friday	Aileen	Alison	Amy	Aster	Johannesburg	Paris	Rome	Tokyo
Madge												
Megan												
Miriam												
Muriel												
Johannesburg												
Paris												
Rome												
Tokyo												
Aileen												
Alison												
Amy												
Aster												

Sender	Day	Friend	City

Dance with Me

Five friends each go to ballroom dancing classes once a week, on a different night from one another. They also drag along their boyfriends, because ballroom dancing requires a partner! Who is each woman's partner and on which evening is their class?

1. Jean and Gerald's dancing class is two evenings before Evelyn's, but the evening after that of Terry and his girlfriend.

2. Gloria and her boyfriend have their class two evenings after Sarah's, but the evening before that of Justin and his girlfriend.

3. Cheryl and her boyfriend Keith don't dance on Friday evenings.

	\multicolumn{5}{c}{Partner}	\multicolumn{5}{c}{Class}
	Gerald	Keith	Justin	Sam	Terry	Monday	Tuesday	Wednesday	Thursday	Friday
Cheryl										
Evelyn										
Gloria										
Jean										
Sarah										
Monday										
Tuesday										
Wednesday										
Thursday										
Friday										

Woman	Partner	Class

Odd Choices

Tammy's four children each have a favorite sandwich, the contents of which are a little strange, to say the least. Can you discover each child's age and his or her preference in terms of first and second ingredients?

1. The child who likes marmalade is one year older than Mary, but younger than the child whose second choice of sandwich filling is salmon.

2. Honey and cheese sandwiches are the preferred choices of the child who is two years older than Carl.

3. Annie is younger than the child whose first choice of sandwich ingredient is peanut butter.

4. The child whose first choice of sandwich ingredient is plum jam never eats cucumber.

	Age				First				Second			
	4	5	6	8	Marmalade	Peanut butter	Plum jam	Honey	Cheese	Cucumber	Egg	Salmon
Annie												
Carl												
Mary												
William												
Cheese												
Cucumber												
Egg												
Salmon												
Marmalade												
Peanut butter												
Plum jam												
Honey												

Child	Age	First	Second

Girls' Toys

Each of the girls in this puzzle had her heart set on a small, inexpensive toy, but none had any money. The girls therefore did small jobs around their homes, in return for payment, until each had saved enough to buy what she wanted. What did each want and what task did each girl undertake?

1. The girl who wanted a ball had saved enough money after cleaning her father's car twice.

2. Elizabeth had set her heart on a splendid new kite, but didn't do the vacuuming in order to earn the money to pay for it.

3. The girl who wanted a spinning top did the shopping, unlike Dina.

4. Suzie did the dusting. Marianne wanted a new doll.

	Toy					Task				
	Ball	Doll	Kite	Jump rope	Spinning top	Cleaning car	Dusting	Gardening	Shopping	Vacuuming
Dina										
Elizabeth										
Katie										
Marianne										
Suzie										
Cleaning car					
Dusting					
Gardening					
Shopping					
Vacuuming					

Girl	Toy	Task

Home Work

Mrs. Gray's five daughters have left home now, but because she is elderly, each visits her once a week to do little tasks for her. Which daughter visits on each of the days listed in the grid below, and what job does she do for her mother?

1. Pam's visit is the day after one of Mrs. Gray's daughters does her washing, but two days before another of her daughters does the cleaning of her house.

2. Vera does Mrs. Gray's ironing later in the week than the visit of the daughter who cooks for her, but earlier in the week than Joanne's visit.

3. Joanne visits her mother the day before Mary's visit.

	Daughter					Job				
	Holly	Joanne	Mary	Pam	Vera	Cleaning	Cooking	Ironing	Shopping	Washing
Mondays										
Tuesdays										
Wednesdays										
Thursdays										
Fridays										
Cleaning										
Cooking										
Ironing										
Shopping										
Washing										

Day	Daughter	Job

Playing to Win

Peter Pawn has just become the youngest-ever U.S. chess grandmaster, having left a trail of opponents defeated in a series of matches across the country. From the clues, can you discover the name of his rival in each city, the time taken to play each game, and the amount of prize money won by Peter?

1. The game against Colin Castle took less time to finish than that against Kurt Knight.

2. Peter won $150 more in Dallas than from his game with Kris King, which took fifteen minutes longer to play than his match in Los Angeles.

3. The longest match to play brought Peter a prize of $450.

	Opponent				Time				Prize			
	Colin Castle	Kris King	Kurt Knight	Ray Rook	50 minutes	60 minutes	65 minutes	75 minutes	$300	$400	$450	$600
Chicago												
Dallas												
Los Angeles												
New York												
$300												
$400												
$450												
$600												
50 minutes												
60 minutes												
65 minutes												
75 minutes												

4. The shortest match took place in Chicago, where Peter didn't win a prize of $400.

5. Peter won more from his match against Ray Rook than from the game that took ten minutes longer to play than the one with Ray Rook.

City	Opponent	Time	Prize

Excuses, Excuses

Brian employs five people, but each missed a day's work last week, for different reasons. On what day did each person fail to turn up for work and what was the reason?

1. The man whose child was sick was away two days later than Adam, who was off work the day after Chris.

2. One man was away from work on Monday to attend a family funeral.

3. Dean's day off work was the day after Eugene's absence due to a stomach ache.

4. Ben was at work all day on Friday.

5. The man who had a migraine wasn't absent on Wednesday.

	Day					Reason				
	Monday	Tuesday	Wednesday	Thursday	Friday	Car problem	Funeral	Migraine	Sick child	Stomach ache
Adam										
Ben										
Chris										
Dean										
Eugene										
Car problem					
Funeral					
Migraine					
Sick child					
Stomach ache					

Employee	Day	Reason

Getting Fit

After putting on rather too much weight in the past few years, Lauren decided to enroll in some fitness classes. She joined four and managed to persuade one friend to enroll in each class, so she'd have someone to go with. The classes are at different times on different days of the week. See if you can do some working out! At what time and on which days are the classes, and which friend accompanies Lauren?

	Time				Day				Friend			
	11:00 A.M.	11:30 A.M.	2:30 P.M.	3:00 P.M.	Mondays	Tuesdays	Wednesdays	Fridays	Babs	Cheryl	Dawn	Erica
Aerobics												
Swimming												
Trampoline												
Yoga												
Babs												
Cheryl												
Dawn												
Erica												
Mondays												
Tuesdays												
Wednesdays												
Fridays												

1. Babs works every morning at a local store, so can only attend afternoon classes.

2. Aerobics classes are held in the morning, two days after Lauren's and Dawn's yoga exercise session.

3. The 2:30 P.M. classes are held on Wednesdays.

4. The classes that start at 11:00 A.M. are held earlier in the week than the swimming classes.

5. Erica doesn't accompany Lauren to trampoline sessions.

Class	Time	Day	Friend

Dog Story

Five of the top prizes in the annual dog show were awarded to those dogs and their owners who appear in this puzzle. Discover the name of the dog that won each prize, as well as that of his proud owner.

1. The dog named Nelson was awarded a prize two places lower than that achieved by Mr. Jones's dog, but higher than that awarded to Miss Neame's animal.

2. Hannibal (who belongs to Mrs. Kent) achieved a position two places higher than that awarded to Mr. O'Connor's dog, but was placed lower than Brutus.

3. Nero won fourth prize for his proud owner.

	Dog					Owner				
	Brutus	Hannibal	Nelson	Nero	Samson	Mr. Jones	Mrs. Kent	Mr. Morris	Miss Neame	Mr. O'Connor
First prize										
Second prize										
Third prize										
Fourth prize										
Fifth prize										
Mr. Jones										
Mrs. Kent										
Mr. Morris										
Miss Neame										
Mr. O'Connor										

Prize	Dog	Owner

Drink Problem

Last week, the four people in this puzzle decided to restock their cellars with beer and wine. Your task is to discover each shopper's surname, together with the amount he or she spent on beer and wine.

1. The shopper surnamed Cooper spent $5 more on wine than on beer.

2. The person who spent $40 on wine spent $5 more on beer than Clarice Fletcher paid for beer.

3. The shopper surnamed Lang spent $35 on wine and $10 less on beer than Jade spent on beer.

4. Anthony's total bill was higher than Nigel's total bill.

	Surname				Beer $				Wine $			
	Cooper	Fletcher	Lang	Vale	30	40	45	50	35	40	45	50
Anthony												
Clarice												
Jade												
Nigel												
Wine $35												
$40												
$45												
$50												
Beer $30												
$40												
$45												
$50												

Shopper	Surname	Beer	Wine

Doggy Dilemma

Four dogs and their owners live in the houses you see on the plan below.
Use the clues to discover where each lives.

1. Bonzo and his owner live farther north than Judy and her dog.

2. Mr. Dawson lives farther west than Fifi and her owner.

3. The person surnamed Williams lives at No. 1.

4. The dog named Sammy belongs to Jenny, whose surname isn't Williams or Brown.

5. Joseph's dog isn't called Wolfie.

	Dog				Owner				Surname			
	Bonzo	Fifi	Sammy	Wolfie	James	Jenny	Joseph	Judy	Brown	Dawson	Smith	Williams
No. 1												
No. 2												
No. 3												
No. 4												
Brown												
Dawson												
Smith												
Williams												
James												
Jenny												
Joseph												
Judy												

N
W   E
S

1   2

3   4

House No.	Dog	Owner	Surname

Potted Plants

There are five pots lined up on the window ledge in Jo's office, acquired in different months of last year. Can you discover not only when they were bought but also the color of the flowers growing in them?

1. The yellow flowers are growing in a pot bought three months later than the pot with white flowers that is directly next to and right of that bought in February.

2. The pot bought in August is farther right than the one with red flowers, which was bought two months earlier than the pot with orange flowers.

3. The pot with blue flowers was bought earlier in the year than pot C.

4. Pot D was bought earlier in the year than pot E.

| | Month | | | | | Flowers | | | |
	February	April	May	July	August	Blue	Orange	Red	White	Yellow
Pot A										
Pot B										
Pot C										
Pot D										
Pot E										
Blue						
Orange						
Red						
White						
Yellow						

LEFT ⇦   RIGHT ⇨

A B C D E

Pot	Month	Flowers

Much-Loved Pets

Josie is emigrating abroad next year and cannot take her pets with her. Luckily, some of her friends and relatives have asked if they could have them, so Josie is overjoyed to have found good homes for them all. What type of creature is each of the named pets and for how long have they enjoyed Josie's affection?

1. Clover has been with Josie for six months longer than the gerbil.

2. Josie has owned the tortoise for two months longer than Marty, but not for as long as Freddie has been with her.

3. Gemma is Josie's cat, who has been with her for less time than her dog, but longer than Topsy.

	Type					Time				
	Cat	Dog	Gerbil	Rabbit	Tortoise	6 months	8 months	10 months	14 months	16 months
Clover										
Freddie										
Gemma										
Marty										
Topsy										
6 months										
8 months										
10 months										
14 months										
16 months										

Name	Type	Time

Recycling

The people in this puzzle all regularly take their used bottles, cans, and newspapers to the recycling center in town. Their most recent visit was this morning, when each took various quantities of all three items. Precisely how many of each item did every person take?

1. John (who took more bottles than papers) took two fewer cans than Maureen.

2. Maureen took two fewer bottles than Lenny.

3. Whoever took 11 cans took one fewer bottle than the person who took nine papers.

4. Karen took the same number of papers as bottles.

5. Whoever took the most cans took two fewer papers than the person who took 12 cans.

	Bottles				Cans				Papers			
	7	8	9	10	10	11	12	13	8	9	10	11
John												
Karen												
Lenny												
Maureen												
8 papers												
9 papers												
10 papers												
11 papers												
10 cans												
11 cans												
12 cans												
13 cans												

Name	Bottles	Cans	Papers

Dorothy's Dates

Next week, Dorothy has five social functions listed in her diary, all of which she intends to attend. Can you discover the time and evening each event is scheduled to take place?

1. The theater trip will take place two evenings after the event that starts at eight o'clock.

2. Dorothy will go bowling on Thursday evening. The bowling event starts 15 minutes later than the dinner party.

3. Bridge club starts at 7:15 P.M., the evening before the dinner party.

	Time					Evening				
	6:45 P.M.	7:15 P.M.	7:30 P.M.	7:45 P.M.	8:00 P.M.	Monday	Tuesday	Wednesday	Thursday	Friday
Bowling										
Fashion show										
Dinner party										
Theater trip										
Bridge club										
Monday										
Tuesday										
Wednesday										
Thursday										
Friday										

Event	Time	Evening

Split Personalities

Jamie took five pictures and cut them each into three pieces (head, body, and legs). He then reassembled them in such a way that each "new" picture contains pieces of three "old" ones. How have the pictures been reassembled?

1. The head of the rhinoceros is in the same picture as the elephant's legs but not the giraffe's body.

2. The head of the elephant is not in the same picture as either the legs or the body of the giraffe.

3. The legs of the cat, the head of the giraffe, and the body of the rhinoceros are in three different pictures.

4. The dog's body is in the same picture as the legs of the rhinoceros but not the elephant's head.

		Body					Legs				
		Cat	Dog	Elephant	Giraffe	Rhinoceros	Cat	Dog	Elephant	Giraffe	Rhinoceros
Head	Cat										
	Dog										
	Elephant										
	Giraffe										
	Rhinoceros										
Legs	Cat										
	Dog										
	Elephant										
	Giraffe										
	Rhinoceros										

Head	Body	Legs

Chairs for Sale

A local auctioneer has four wooden chairs among the furniture for sale tomorrow—not just any old chairs, as these were made by renowned furniture-makers of the early 19th century. Which craftsman made each chair (they are set out as per the picture below), when was it made, and of which type of wood?

1. The chair made of oak is next to and right of the one made by Heppel eight years before the chair made by Whyte (which is farther left than the chair made by Heppel).

	Maker				Year				Wood			
	Chipp	Dale	Heppel	Whyte	1815	1819	1823	1827	Beech	Mahogany	Oak	Walnut
Chair A												
Chair B												
Chair C												
Chair D												
Beech												
Mahogany												
Oak												
Walnut												
1815												
1819												
1823												
1827												

LEFT ⇐   RIGHT ⇒

A B C D

2. The beech chair was made four years earlier than the walnut chair, which isn't chair B. The beech chair wasn't made by Heppel.

3. One of the chairs was made in 1823 by Adolphus Chipp. It is next to and right of the chair made in 1819.

4. Chair A wasn't made by Dale.

Chair	Maker	Year	Wood

Halloween Party

Everyone who was invited to Jodi and Jim's Halloween party was asked to dress in costume, and the first five guests to arrive all came dressed as something different. Can you work out what each chose to wear and the order in which he or she arrived?

1. Katie dressed as a witch and arrived (by taxi, not on a broomstick!) earlier than the person dressed in bandages to look like an Egyptian mummy, but later than Paul.

2. Laura arrived later than the person dressed as a ghost, who arrived later than Joe.

3. Martin was the first guest to arrive at Jodi and Jim's Halloween party, but not in a vampire's costume.

	Costume					Order				
	Ghost	Mummy	Skeleton	Vampire	Witch	First	Second	Third	Fourth	Fifth
Joe										
Katie										
Laura										
Martin										
Paul										
First										
Second										
Third										
Fourth										
Fifth										

Guest	Costume	Order

Dates and Times

Four men who share an apartment all had dates last night and left at different times to take buses to their destinations. Can you determine the time at which each friend left the house, the number of the bus he took, and his destination?

	Time				Bus No.				Destination			
	7:00 P.M.	7:15 P.M.	7:30 P.M.	7:40 P.M.	16	29	42	55	Cinema	Nightclub	Restaurant	Theater
Benny												
Denny												
Kenny												
Lenny												
Cinema												
Nightclub												
Restaurant												
Theater												
Bus No. 16												
Bus No. 29												
Bus No. 42												
Bus No. 55												

1. Benny (who wasn't the first man to leave the apartment) took a bus with a number twenty-six higher than that taken by the man who went to the theater.

2. The man who took his date to the theater left the apartment a quarter of an hour later than the one who took his date to the nightclub.

3. The man who went to the nightclub took a bus with a lower number than that taken by Denny, who left the apartment earlier than Kenny, who took his date to the restaurant.

4. Kenny left the apartment earlier than the man who took the number 55 bus.

Man	Time	Bus No.	Dest'n

Easter Egg Hunt

All of the children who took part in the Annual Egg Hunt last Easter found a number of little eggs, but the five who are taking part in this puzzle found more than anyone else. What was the color of each child's basket and how many eggs did he or she find?

1. The child with the brown basket found two fewer eggs than Danny, who found fewer than Ivan, who didn't have the yellow basket.

2. Edgar found three fewer eggs than the child with the purple basket, who found fewer than Henry.

3. The child with the scarlet basket found one fewer egg than the child whose basket was yellow, but more eggs than Gordon discovered.

	Basket					No. Found				
	Brown	Green	Purple	Scarlet	Yellow	12	14	15	17	18
Danny										
Edgar										
Gordon										
Henry										
Ivan										
12 eggs					
14 eggs					
15 eggs					
17 eggs					
18 eggs					

Child	Basket	No. Found

Proud Parents

Four couples are each celebrating the arrival of their first child, born yesterday. Can you match each couple to their child and the time he or she was born?

1. Daniel was born three hours before Gregory's first child (who isn't called Susan), but later than Linda's baby.

2. Barbara's baby was born in the afternoon and Jerry's child was born in the morning; both babies are girls.

3. Walter and his wife Elizabeth didn't name their child Paul. Paul was the last baby of the day to be born.

	Barbara	Elizabeth	Linda	Rebecca	Daniel	Maria	Paul	Susan	8:00 A.M.	11:00 A.M.	2:00 P.M.	5:00 P.M.
Andrew												
Gregory												
Jerry												
Walter												
8:00 A.M.												
11:00 A.M.												
2:00 P.M.												
5:00 P.M.												
Daniel												
Maria												
Paul												
Susan												

Father (rows), Time, Child labels at left.

Father	Mother	Child	Time

Island Traders

The four islands you see on the map below are occupied by different tribes (each of which has a name that starts with the same letter as that by which their islands are identified on the map). Their merchants travel from one island to each of the other three, visiting every island once per year, but not their own, of course! Discover which island was visited by each island's merchants in the listed months of 2009.

1. The Baleran merchants visited island C later in the year than island D.

2. The island visited by the Daconian merchants in April is farther south than the one they visited in July.

3. One group of merchants sailed to island B in April and island C in July.

4. The Calieri merchants didn't travel south in April (except to return home!).

	April				July				October			
	A	B	C	D	A	B	C	D	A	B	C	D
Armosians												
Balerans												
Calieris												
Daconians												

October
A				
B				
C				
D				

July
A				
B				
C				
D				

Tribe	April	July	October

N
W — E
S

A
B
C
D

Dates

Five sisters each dated five different boys last week, coincidentally all brothers! Who dated whom and on which night of the week?

1. Joanne's date was the night after Martin's and the night before Terry's.

2. Alan's date was the night before Sylvia's and the night after Kate's.

3. Pamela's date (which wasn't on Monday) was the night before Veronica's.

4. Veronica's date wasn't with Carl.

	Brother					Night				
	Alan	Carl	Martin	Peter	Terry	Monday	Tuesday	Wednesday	Thursday	Friday
Joanne										
Kate										
Pamela										
Sylvia										
Veronica										
Monday					
Tuesday					
Wednesday					
Thursday					
Friday					

Sister	Brother	Night

Gifts

When she was recently in the hospital, Greta received a visit from each of her four cousins, every one of whom bought her a small gift to keep her occupied, which was wrapped in paper and adorned with a bow. Can you discover what each presented to Greta, together with the color of the bow and the paper in which it was wrapped?

	Gift				Paper				Bow			
	Book	Embroidery set	Jigsaw puzzle	Knitting items	Blue	Pink	Purple	White	Orange	Red	Turquoise	Yellow
Denise												
Larry												
Michael												
Roberta												
Orange												
Red												
Turquoise												
Yellow												
Blue												
Pink												
Purple												
White												

(Left side labels: Bow — Orange, Red, Turquoise, Yellow; Paper — Blue, Pink, Purple, White)

Cousin	Gift	Paper	Bow

1. The orange bow adorned the parcel wrapped in snowy white paper, which was given to Greta by one of the women.

2. The book wasn't the present wrapped in pink paper, which was given to Greta by Larry.

3. The jigsaw puzzle, the gift with a turquoise bow, and the one wrapped in blue paper were presented by three different cousins, none of whom is Denise.

4. The embroidery set was wrapped in purple paper adorned with a yellow bow.

Pre-loved Cars

Four men have each bought a secondhand car today and are very pleased with their purchases. What make of car did each buy and what is its age and color?

1. The white car is one year older than the green car.

2. Liam purchased the Teant, which isn't as old as the Marita.

3. The Marita is older than the car purchased by Kirk, but newer than the gray car.

4. Melvyn bought the blue car, which is two years older than the Arravo.

	Make				Age				Color			
	Arravo	Marita	Skorder	Teant	2 years	3 years	4 years	5 years	Blue	Green	Gray	White
Jack												
Kirk												
Liam												
Melvyn												
Blue								
Green								
Gray								
White								
2 years				
3 years				
4 years				
5 years				

Buyer	Make	Age	Color

Drinks All Around

The diagram below shows a table in a local bar, at which five friends are seated, each with a different drink. Can you discover the name of the occupant of each seat, together with his or her drink of choice?

1. Looking clockwise around the table, not necessarily starting from seat A, we see: Daniel; the person with a martini; the one drinking coffee; Simon; and Claire.

2. Brian is seated next to and between Moira and the person with a tall glass of lemonade.

3. The person in seat A isn't drinking beer. The man in seat B is drinking iced mineral water.

	Brian	Claire	Daniel	Moira	Simon	Beer	Coffee	Lemonade	Martini	Mineral water
Seat A										
Seat B										
Seat C										
Seat D										
Seat E										
Beer										
Coffee										
Lemonade										
Martini										
Mineral water										

CLOCKWISE

Seat	Occupant	Drink

Damages

Last week was a bad one for the household moving company, Stumble and Fawl. They only had four bookings, but on each job they managed to break an item beyond repair. On which day was each person's property moved, what valuable item was broken, and how much did it cost to replace?

1. The clock was broken earlier in the week than Mr. Dean's item, but later in the week than the object that cost $100 more to replace than Mr. Dean's item.

2. Mrs. Player's antique lamp cost more to replace than the item broken on Tuesday, but less than the object belonging to Ms. Byron.

3. The vase cost $50 more to replace than the table.

	Day				Item				Cost			
	Monday	Tuesday	Wednesday	Friday	Clock	Lamp	Table	Vase	$150	$200	$250	$300
Ms. Byron												
Mr. Dean												
Mrs. Ford												
Mrs. Player												
$150												
$200												
$250												
$300												
Clock												
Lamp												
Table												
Vase												

Owner	Day	Item	Cost

Celebratory Cruises

Five couples celebrating their Golden Wedding Anniversaries have each booked a place on a luxury liner to an exotic location. Can you pair up the listed husbands and wives, then discover their destinations?

1. Dora and her husband Ronnie haven't booked the cruise to South America, nor the one to Australasia.

2. Theo's wife isn't Thelma or Eileen; and Eileen's husband isn't Bill.

3. The couple booked on the Australasian cruise are neither Peter and his wife nor Thelma and her husband (who isn't Peter).

4. Rachel and her husband are looking forward to cruising the Mediterranean just as much as Theo and his wife are looking forward to cruising the Pacific Islands.

	Christine	Dora	Eileen	Rachel	Thelma	Australasia	Indian Ocean	Mediterranean	Pacific Islands	South America
Bill										
Malcolm										
Peter										
Ronnie										
Theo										
Australasia										
Indian Ocean										
Mediterranean										
Pacific Islands										
South America										

Husband	Wife	Destination

Getting to Work

Four employees of the NBA Insurance Company take various lengths of time to get to work every morning. Can you identify each employee by his or her full name, job in the company, and the time it takes him or her to get to work?

	Surname				Position				Time (minutes)			
	Johnson	Miller	Parry	Raille	Asst. Manager	Chief Teller	Manager	Secretary	15	17	20	23
Charles												
Hazel												
Jeremy												
Trina												
15 minutes												
17 minutes												
20 minutes												
23 minutes												
Asst. Manager												
Chief Teller												
Manager												
Secretary												

1. Mr. Johnson takes longer to travel to work than Trina, but less time than the Chief Teller.

2. Charles takes three minutes longer to get to work than the employee surnamed Raille.

3. The Manager's surname is Miller. He or she takes longer to travel to work than the Assistant Manager.

4. The Secretary takes less time to travel to work than the Assistant Manager.

Employee	Surname	Position	Time

In the Garden

Five enthusiastic gardeners spent a lot of time digging, weeding, and planting in their gardens last weekend. Can you discover just how many hours each worked on Saturday and Sunday?

1. On Saturday, Bert spent longer in the garden than Gerda, but on Sunday, both he and Brian spent less time in the garden than Gerda.

2. Bill spent one hour longer in the garden on Sunday than on Saturday.

3. Gina spent one hour less time working in the garden on Sunday than she had done on Saturday.

4. Brian spent exactly the same amount of time in the garden on Sunday as he had done on Saturday.

5. Whoever worked the longest time in the garden on Saturday didn't put in the fewest hours' work on Sunday.

	Saturday					Sunday				
	4 hours	4½ hours	5 hours	6 hours	6½ hours	3 hours	3½ hours	4½ hours	5 hours	6 hours
Bert										
Bill										
Brian										
Gerda										
Gina										
3 hours										
3½ hours										
4½ hours										
5 hours										
6 hours										

Gardener	Saturday	Sunday

Royal Ancestors

Prince Rupert of Royaltania is learning about his ancestors. Can you discover which king ruled Royaltania in the years listed in the grid below, together with the name of the queen?

1. King Albert's reign was longer than that of the man married to Queen Charlotte, but not as long as the reign of Queen Henrietta and her husband.

2. King David's reign was earlier than that of the man married to Queen Charlotte.

3. Queen Anne's husband wasn't King Steven, whose reign was later than that of the man married to Queen Henrietta.

4. King Michael's reign was later than (but not directly after) that of Queen Tabitha and her husband.

	King					Queen				
	Albert	Alfonso	David	Michael	Steven	Anne	Charlotte	Henrietta	Margaret	Tabitha
1802–16										
1816–24										
1824–50										
1850–76										
1876–90										
Anne										
Charlotte										
Henrietta										
Margaret										
Tabitha										

Years	King	Queen

Mountain Men

Five members of a mountaineering club decided to go their separate ways this year and headed teams to climb different mountains. How many years' experience has each climber and which mountain did he conquer?

1. Eric, who successfully led a team up Mount McKinley, has two more years' experience than the man who climbed Mount Rainier.

2. The mountaineer who tackled Mount Hood has more years' experience than Frank, but not as many years' experience as the man who led his party to the summit of El Capitan.

3. Mount Foraker was the choice of Burt, who has four more years' experience than Dennis.

	Experience					Mountain				
	5 years	6 years	7 years	9 years	10 years	El Capitan	Mt. Foraker	Mt. Hood	Mt. McKinley	Mt. Rainier
Alan										
Burt										
Dennis										
Eric										
Frank										
El Capitan										
Mt. Foraker										
Mt. Hood										
Mt. McKinley										
Mt. Rainier										

Name	Experience	Mountain

Model-Making

Four teachers decided to hold a model-making session at school, having asked their pupils to bring in cardboard boxes and tubes that could be used to make the models. Discover the full name of each teacher and the quantities of boxes and tubes collected by their pupils.

1. The pupils of the teacher surnamed Hope brought in as many tubes as the number of boxes collected by the pupils of the teacher surnamed Smith.

2. Roger's pupils brought in six fewer tubes than the number of boxes collected by the pupils of another teacher, whose surname is Barton.

3. Laura's pupils collected both two more boxes and two more tubes than Sarah's.

4. One teacher's pupils brought in a total of 48 tubes and 54 boxes.

	Surname				Boxes				Tubes			
	Barton	Hope	Lawson	Smith	48	50	54	56	42	46	48	50
Laura												
Pete												
Roger												
Sarah												
42 tubes												
46 tubes												
48 tubes												
50 tubes												
48 boxes												
50 boxes												
54 boxes												
56 boxes												

Teacher	Surname	Boxes	Tubes

Flower Finder

Flora Flinders was an early 20th-century botanist and explorer who brought back five hitherto unknown flowering plants when she returned home to the USA in 1907. From the clues, can you discover the color of each flower (named in honor of a town in her native state of Wyoming) and its native habitat?

1. Baggsia is a plant only to be found in mountainous regions in the wild, unlike the plant with vibrant scarlet flowers. The plant with scarlet flowers is never to be found in a swamp.

2. The orange blooms of the desert-loving plant appear only once every ten years.

3. Torringtona has fragrant, bright yellow flowers that hang in clusters along its slender stems. Neither Laderia nor Torringtona grows in the forest.

4. The plant with pale pink flowers is taller and hardier than the swamp-loving plant, Aftonia.

	Orange	Pink	Purple	Scarlet	Yellow	Desert	Forest	Mountain	Seashore	Swamp
Aftonia										
Baggsia										
Laderia										
Storysia										
Torringtona										
Desert										
Forest										
Mountain										
Seashore										
Swamp										

Plant	Flower	Habitat

Car Repairs

The four cars in the diagram below are lined up at a local garage, waiting for repairs. Can you discover each car's type, the repair it needs, and the name of its owner?

1. There is a dent in the hood of Alice's vehicle, which is parked somewhere between the convertible and the coupé.

2. The car that needs to have its headlights adjusted is directly next to Roger's vehicle.

3. Car C is the pickup, which doesn't have a dent or a rust hole.

4. Roger's car is farther left than the convertible.

5. The car with the faulty trunk lock isn't parked next to Stephanie's vehicle.

	Type				Repair				Owner			
	Convertible	Coupé	Pickup	Sedan	Dent	Headlights	Rust hole	Trunk lock	Alice	Roger	Stephanie	Thomas
Car A												
Car B												
Car C												
Car D												
Alice												
Roger												
Stephanie												
Thomas												
Dent												
Headlights												
Rust hole												
Trunk lock												

LEFT ⇐   RIGHT ⇒

A B C D

Car	Type	Repair	Owner

Birds, Trees, and Flowers

Four children have painted elaborate pictures of their gardens, filling them with birds, trees, and flowers. Can you decide how many of each feature in the five paintings?

1. The picture with the most flowers has two more trees than birds.

2. Florence's picture has fewer flowers than trees. The number of birds that feature in Elizabeth's picture is different than the number of trees in Florence's picture.

3. Graham's picture has fewer flowers than Elizabeth's, but more flowers than that painted by David.

4. Elizabeth's picture has more birds than David's. David's painting doesn't have one fewer tree than Graham's.

5. The picture with the fewest trees doesn't have the most birds.

	Birds				Trees				Flowers			
	2	3	5	6	2	3	4	5	2	4	5	6
David												
Elizabeth												
Florence												
Graham												
2 flowers												
4 flowers												
5 flowers												
6 flowers												
2 trees												
3 trees												
4 trees												
5 trees												

Child	Birds	Trees	Flowers

Parsley, Sage, Rosemary, and Thyme

The four jars you see below all contain a different herb. Moreover, no jar is of the same color as that of its lid; so pick your way through the clues to identify them all.

1. The jar of parsley is next to and left of the blue jar, which is next to and left of the one with the blue lid.

2. The red lid isn't on the violet jar, which is next to and left of the red jar, which is next to and left of the one containing thyme.

3. The green jar doesn't contain sage.

	Herb				Jar Color				Lid Color			
	Parsley	Rosemary	Sage	Thyme	Blue	Green	Red	Violet	Blue	Green	Red	Violet
Jar A												
Jar B												
Jar C												
Jar D												
Lid Color Blue												
Green												
Red												
Violet												
Jar Color Blue												
Green												
Red												
Violet												

LEFT ⇐   RIGHT ⇒

A   B   C   D

Jar	Herb	Jar	Lid

Church Funds

The town of Mitchburg has four old churches, all in need of repair. The priest of each church organized a different event to raise funds for renovations. The events were all well attended by the people of the town, and you can discover the name of the priest at each church, the event he organized, and the amount it raised, from the clues below!

	Priest				Event				Amount			
	Rev. Frazer	Rev. Glade	Rev. Stone	Rev. White	Auction	Church sale	Dance	Sports day	$1,200	$1,700	$2,200	$2,700
St. Andrew's												
St. John's												
St. Mary's												
St. Paul's												
$1,200												
$1,700												
$2,200												
$2,700												
Auction												
Church sale												
Dance												
Sports day												

1. Reverend Frazer's event raised more money than the dance, but not as much as the event organized by the priest at St. John's (who isn't Reverend Glade).

2. The event held in aid of funds for the restoration of the paths at St. Mary's raised more money than that organized by Reverend Stone, but not as much as the sports day.

3. The priest at St. Paul's who organized the church sale raised more money than Reverend White.

Church	Priest	Event	Amount

Monday Quiz

Another episode in the long-running TV game show series *Monday Quiz* is about to start and four hopeful contestants are lined up at the consoles as shown in the diagram below, waiting to be introduced and to take part in the show. What is the first name and surname of each contestant and where does he or she live?

1. The contestant from Eastwood is next to and between Ian and the person surnamed Thorne.

2. Hope is farther left than Ian, but farther right than the contestant surnamed Richardson, who is from Southville.

3. Jill Potter is farther left than the contestant from West Hill.

	First name				Surname				Town			
	Hope	Ian	Jill	Keith	Potter	Richardson	Stockton	Thorne	Eastwood	North Bay	Southville	West Hill
Console A												
Console B												
Console C												
Console D												
Eastwood												
North Bay												
Southville												
West Hill												
Potter												
Richardson												
Stockton												
Thorne												

LEFT ⇐   RIGHT ⇒

A   B   C   D

Console	Name	Surname	Town

Cats' Tale

Five cats and their owners live in houses in Kittyville. Can you discover the feline facts? The clues and the map below should help.

1. Caesar lives in a house with a number one higher than that owned by Nigel, who lives directly north of Norman.

2. Duke's owner lives directly east of Naomi and her cat.

3. Nancy lives farther south and farther west than Sam's owner.

4. Ned and his cat Lucky don't live directly west of Norman.

| | Cat | | | | | Owner | | | | |
	Caesar	Duke	Felix	Lucky	Sam	Nancy	Naomi	Ned	Nigel	Norman
No. 1										
No. 2										
No. 3										
No. 4										
No. 5										
Nancy										
Naomi										
Ned										
Nigel										
Norman										

House No.	Cat	Owner

Ski Vacation

Four sisters met to talk about their recent ski vacations in Canada. Where did each sister spend her vacation, how long did she stay, and which particular sport is her favorite?

1. Vicky spent most of her time on her snowboard, a sport she prefers to all others. Her vacation was longer than Teri's.

2. The sister who spent her vacation in the wonderful resort of Whistler prefers the ski jump.

3. Tessa's vacation was longer than that of the woman who went to Kicking Horse, but not as long as that of the Langlauf lover.

4. Slalom is the favorite sport of the woman whose vacation (not at Mount Cain) lasted for ten days.

	Kicking Horse	Lake Louise	Mount Cain	Whistler	7 days	9 days	10 days	14 days	Langlauf	Ski jump	Slalom	Snowboard
Lavinia												
Teri												
Tessa												
Vicky												
Langlauf												
Ski jump												
Slalom												
Snowboard												
7 days												
9 days												
10 days												
14 days												

Sister	Resort	Stay	Sport

Recycled Rubbish

The four women in this puzzle are all concerned with salvaging and recycling waste material. Every woman collects a particular type of discarded material from her neighbors and takes it to the recycling depot once a week. What does each collect, which day does she go to the depot, and how many bags of rubbish did she take last week?

	Material				Day				Bags			
	Aluminum	Glass	Paper	Plastic	Monday	Tuesday	Wednesday	Thursday	12	15	18	21
Amanda												
Debra												
Martha												
Pamela												
12 bags												
15 bags												
18 bags												
21 bags												
Monday												
Tuesday												
Wednesday												
Thursday												

1. The waste aluminum (mostly empty cans) is taken to the depot the day before Martha's trip.

2. Last week, one woman took three more bags of plastic on Tuesday than the number of bags of paper taken by Pamela, whose trip to the depot wasn't on Monday.

3. The highest number of bags was taken to the depot, but not by Amanda, earlier in the week than the bags of glass bottles and jars.

4. Debra took 12 bags to the depot last week, two days before the bags of glass were taken.

Collector	Material	Day	Bags

New Homes

Four newly married couples moved into their new homes in Newtown last week. Can you discover who is married to whom, their surname, and the day on which they took up residence?

1. Dean and his wife moved in the day before Sandra and her husband, who moved in earlier in the week than Mr. & Mrs. Hopwood.

2. Mr. & Mrs. Jarvis moved in earlier in the week than the Nortons, but later in the week than Ian and his wife, Thelma.

3. Hannah's surname isn't Jarvis.

4. Hannah's husband isn't Richard.

	Wife				Surname				Day			
	Alice	Hannah	Sandra	Thelma	Hopwood	Jarvis	Norton	Pringle	Tuesday	Wednesday	Thursday	Saturday
Dean												
Ian												
Mike												
Richard												
Tuesday												
Wednesday												
Thursday												
Saturday												
Hopwood												
Jarvis												
Norton												
Pringle												

Husband	Wife	Surname	Day

Tennis Players

Five members of the Court family played tennis yesterday morning and each managed to play two sets before bad weather forced them to stop. How many games did each member of the family play and win against his or her opponents?

1. Peter won three games in the first set and Steven won four games in the second set.

2. The number of games won by Steven in the first set is the same as the number won by Veronica in the second set.

3. The number of games won by Veronica in the first set is the same as the number won by Peter in the second set.

4. Thelma won three fewer games in the second set than she had in the first set.

5. In total, Jane won exactly the same number of games as Peter.

	1st Set					2nd Set				
	3	4	5	6	7	3	4	5	6	7
Jane										
Peter										
Steven										
Thelma										
Veronica										

2nd Set						
	3					
	4					
	5					
	6					
	7					

Player	1st Set	2nd Set

Vitamin Supplements

Julie regularly takes vitamin supplements in the form of pills. At different times this morning, she took a pill, but can you digest the information below to discover the color of the pill she took at the times listed, the vitamin it contains, and the drink she used to wash it down?

1. The vitamin K pill (which isn't red) was taken with a glass of milk two hours later than the vitamin A pill.

2. Julie had a glass of apple juice with the pill she took at half past seven this morning. This wasn't the blue pill, which she took earlier than the vitamin C pill.

3. The brown pill was taken one hour after the pill that Julie swallowed with water, but earlier than the red pill.

	Color				Vitamin				Drink			
	Blue	Brown	Red	White	A	C	E	K	Apple juice	Coffee	Milk	Water
7:30 A.M.												
8:30 A.M.												
9:30 A.M.												
11:30 A.M.												
Apple juice												
Coffee												
Milk												
Water												
Vitamin A												
Vitamin C												
Vitamin E												
Vitamin K												

Time	Color	Vitamin	Drink

Playtime

Five little girls are busy dressing their dolls, each in two different colors, neither of which begin with the same letter as that of her name. In which two colors has each girl chosen to dress her doll?

1. Gloria's doll is being put into a jacket of the same color as the dress chosen by Briony for her doll.

2. Polly's doll has a jacket of the same color as that of the dress picked by Tina for her doll to wear.

3. The doll that is being clothed in a red dress and blue jacket doesn't belong to Polly.

4. The doll that will be wearing a blue dress and pink jacket when fully clothed doesn't belong to Rosemary.

5. No doll will be wearing both a pink dress and a turquoise jacket.

	Dress					Jacket				
	Blue	Green	Pink	Red	Turquoise	Blue	Green	Pink	Red	Turquoise
Briony										
Gloria										
Polly										
Rosemary										
Tina										
Blue										
Green										
Pink										
Red										
Turquoise										

Jacket

Girl	Dress	Jacket

Shopping Spree

Douglas and Diane are setting up house together and went shopping yesterday to buy a few items. Discover the order in which they went into each shop, together with the name of the assistant who served them and the item they bought there.

1. Jennifer was the assistant at the store visited directly before Douglas and Diane went to Arkwright's, where they purchased an oven.

2. Michael (who works in Home Help) assisted the couple directly after they were served in Wise Buys.

3. Douglas and Diane bought a table in the third store they visited, where they weren't served by Jennifer or William.

4. The drapes weren't purchased from Capital K.

	Order				Assistant				Purchase			
	First	Second	Third	Fourth	Jennifer	Michael	Nancy	William	Drapes	Oven	Table	Teapot
Arkwright's												
Capital K												
Home Help												
Wise Buys												
Drapes												
Oven												
Table												
Teapot												
Jennifer												
Michael												
Nancy												
William												

Shop	Order	Assistant	Purchase

The Boys in the Band

Since their formation in the early part of last year, the band with the unlovely name of The Frogspots had a steady turnover of members, all eager for fame but talentless. However, for the past few months their audiences have increased, and the current members of the band are working well together. See if you can work out each member's real name (not so "cool" as his stage name!), his position in the band, and the length of time he has been with The Frogspots.

	Real name				Position				Months			
	Arthur	Charles	Edward	William	Bass guitarist	Drummer	Lead guitarist	Singer	6	7	8	9
Animal												
Butch												
Shiner												
Wild Man												
6 months												
7 months												
8 months												
9 months												
Bass guitarist												
Drummer												
Lead guitarist												
Singer												

Name	Real name	Position	Months

1. Edward (who isn't Shiner) has been with The Frogspots for two fewer months than Animal, who isn't the bass guitarist.

2. Butch is the lead guitarist and has been a member of The Frogspots for longer than the bass guitarist but for one fewer month than William.

3. Charles is better known as Wild Man to his fans and has been with the band for less time than the singer, better known as Shiner.

Bunch of Dates

Four friends were all born on different dates in different months. How old is each and on which date does she celebrate her birthday?

1. Joanne is two years older than the woman whose birthday falls six days earlier in its month than Jane's.

2. The 23-year-old celebrates her birthday four months after that of the woman born on the 22nd.

3. Judy (who wasn't born on the 10th) celebrates her birthday in August.

4. Jenny is older than the woman who was born on the 10th.

	Age				Date				Month			
	20	22	23	24	10th	13th	16th	22nd	April	June	August	October
Jane												
Jenny												
Joanne												
Judy												
April												
June												
August												
October												
10th												
13th												
16th												
22nd												

Friend	Age	Date	Month

Wrapping Up Warm

It's very cold today, so four friends are dressed in hats, coats, and scarves. However, everyone is wearing three different colors. Use the clues below to discover which color of hat, coat, and scarf each friend is wearing.

1. The woman in the apricot-colored coat isn't wearing anything blue.

2. Lynne is wearing a pink hat, but not the lime green scarf.

3. The woman in the blue coat and apricot-colored scarf has a shorter name than that of the woman who is dressed in the pink scarf.

4. Paula's scarf isn't blue.

	Coat				Hat				Scarf			
	Apricot	Blue	Lime	Pink	Apricot	Blue	Lime	Pink	Apricot	Blue	Lime	Pink
Lynne												
Martine												
Olga												
Paula												
Scarf Apricot												
Blue												
Lime												
Pink												
Hat Apricot												
Blue												
Lime												
Pink												

Friend	Hat	Coat	Scarf

Split Personalities

In a fit of pique on finding out that superheroes he admired are all fictional, Robin cut pictures of five of them into three pieces (head, body, and legs), then reassembled them in such a way that each "new" picture contains pieces of three "old" ones. How have the pictures been reassembled?

1. The body of Buck Rogers now has Superman's head but not Batman's legs.

2. Batman's body isn't in the same picture as either the head or legs of Buck Rogers.

3. Iceman's head is now attached to Spider-Man's body.

4. Spider-Man's legs are in the same picture as Batman's head but not Superman's body.

		Body					Legs				
		Batman	Buck Rogers	Iceman	Spider-Man	Superman	Batman	Buck Rogers	Iceman	Spider-Man	Superman
Head	Batman										
	Buck Rogers										
	Iceman										
	Spider-Man										
	Superman										
Legs	Batman										
	Buck Rogers										
	Iceman										
	Spider-Man										
	Superman										

Head	Body	Legs

Fully Insured

Four people each paid their annual premiums for car insurance, health insurance, and home insurance over the course of the final five months of last year. No one paid more than one premium per month, so use the clues below to find out when each paid.

1. Cheryl paid her car insurance the month before James paid his health insurance (which was the same month that Sophie paid her home insurance).

2. Graham paid his health insurance earlier in the year than his home insurance, but later in the year than his car insurance.

3. The person who paid for home insurance in November also paid for car insurance in December.

	Car Insurance				Health Insurance				Home Insurance			
	August	September	November	December	August	September	October	December	August	October	November	December
Cheryl												
Graham												
James												
Sophie												
Home August												
Home October												
Home November												
Home December												
Health August												
Health September												
Health October												
Health December												

Name	Car	Health	Home

Spelling Test

In a recent spelling test at school, the five children in this puzzle did particularly badly! What are their full names and how many spellings (out of a total of twenty) did each get wrong?

1. The boy surnamed Carter made three fewer spelling mistakes than the number made by Cora.

2. Sally made fewer spelling mistakes than Jim Robertson, but more than the child surnamed Adams, who isn't Larry.

3. The child surnamed Willard made one fewer mistake than the child surnamed Evans.

4. Larry made fewer mistakes than Brian.

	Adams	Carter	Evans	Robertson	Willard	8	9	11	12	14
Brian										
Cora										
Jim										
Larry										
Sally										
8 mistakes					
9 mistakes					
11 mistakes					
12 mistakes					
14 mistakes					

Child	Surname	Mistakes

Where Do They Live?

Four friends of different ages live in the houses you see on the map below. You can discover their full names, where they live, and their ages by following the clues.

1. Maggie is one year older than the girl who lives at No. 3.

2. Miss Goodman lives in a house farther west than Rosie's home.

3. The 11-year-old lives farther south than Miss Harper.

4. Sue Ireland is two years younger than the girl who lives at No. 1.

5. Miss Forbes (who doesn't live at No. 4) is older than Ellen.

	Surname				House No.				Age			
	Forbes	Goodman	Harper	Ireland	1	2	3	4	9	10	11	12
Ellen												
Maggie												
Rosie												
Sue												
9												
10												
11												
12												
No. 1												
No. 2												
No. 3												
No. 4												

N W E S

| 1 | | 2 |
| 3 | | 4 |

Name	Surname	House No.	Age

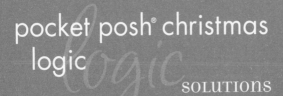

pocket posh® christmas logic

SOLUTIONS

1

The capture at the Golden Oak was in 1887 (clue 2), so that at Pedro's was in 1885 (clue 1) and the posse of 29 men led by Mitch Murphy made a capture in 1882. Bill Barnes's was thus in 1885 (2) and Eddie Hill's in 1887. Sam Peters's capture was thus in 1884. He had 38 men (3), so Eddie Hill had 42 (2) and Bill Barnes had 33. Sam Peters went to the Silver Steer (3) and Mitch Murphy went to the Lazy K.

Thus:

Bill Barnes - Pedro's - 33 - 1885;
Eddie Hill - Golden Oak - 42 - 1887;
Mitch Murphy - Lazy K - 29 - 1882;
Sam Peters - Silver Steer - 38 - 1884.

2

Remember throughout the values of the playing cards (intro). Paul has either the 2 or 10 of spades (clue 1), as has Raymond (clue 2). The man with the 4 of clubs isn't Jeff (1), Raymond (2), or Norman (4), so Paul. Paul's diamond isn't the queen or king (3), so Paul has the 4 of diamonds (2) and Raymond has the 2 of spades. Jeff has the jack of clubs (1) and Paul has the 10 of spades. Norman has the 7 of diamonds (4) and the 10 of clubs, so Raymond has the 3 of clubs. Paul has the 4 of diamonds (above), so (by elimination) Jeff has the king of diamonds and (3) 7 of spades. Norman has the ace of spades and Raymond has the queen of diamonds.

Thus (club - diamond - spade):

Jeff - jack - king - 7;
Norman - 10 - 7 - ace;
Paul - 4 - 4 - 10;
Raymond - 3 - queen - 2.

3

No dinner party started at 7:30 P.M. (grid), so the dinner party on the 6th started at 7:45 P.M. (clue 4), when education was discussed. Margaret's dinner party thus started at 7:15 P.M. (clue 1) and politics was discussed at the dinner party which started at 7:00 P.M. Religion was discussed at Margaret's dinner party (4). Health was discussed on the 20th (5). Margaret's dinner party wasn't on the 13th (3), so the 27th. Helen's started at 8:00 P.M. (2). Charles's was on the 13th (3) and (by elimination) the topic discussed at Charles's dinner party was politics. Patrick's dinner party was on the 6th.

Thus:

Charles - 13th - 7:00 P.M. - politics;
Helen - 20th - 8:00 P.M. - health;
Margaret - 27th - 7:15 P.M. - religion;
Patrick - 6th - 7:45 P.M. - education.

4

The man (thus either Martin or Stephen) who plays the oboe and listens to Handel (clue 2) isn't surnamed Border, so the man surnamed Border listens to Mahler (clue 1). Thus Border is the tuba player (3) and Penny's surname is Moore. By elimination, the women play the piano and violin, and listen to Brahms and Mozart, so Stephen's surname is Wilson (4) and the violinist listens to Brahms. By elimination, the pianist listens to Mozart, and Martin's surname is Border, so Stephen plays the oboe. Dawn's surname is (by elimination) Jacobs. She doesn't play the piano (1), so the violin. Penny plays the piano.

Thus:

Dawn - Jacobs - violin - Brahms;
Martin - Border - tuba - Mahler;
Penny - Moore - piano - Mozart;
Stephen - Wilson - oboe - Handel.

5

Remember throughout that each picture is made up of parts of three different pictures (intro). Nora's grandpa's body is with her cousin's legs (clue 1), so not her cousin's head. Her uncle's head is with her sister's body (clue 2). Her uncle's legs and cousin's head (3) aren't with her uncle's body (intro), so her aunt's body. Her grandpa's head isn't with her cousin's body (1), so her grandpa's head is with her uncle's body, but not her sister's legs (2), so her aunt's legs. By elimination, her sister's legs are with her aunt's head and cousin's body, her sister's head is with her grandpa's body and cousin's legs, and her uncle's head is with her grandpa's legs.

Thus (head - body - legs):

Aunt - cousin - sister;
Cousin - aunt - uncle;
Grandpa - uncle - aunt;
Sister - grandpa - cousin;
Uncle - sister - grandpa.

6

The 4:00 P.M. appointment was with a woman whose hair isn't silver (clue 1), blonde (clue 2), brown, or chestnut (3), so black. The silver-haired woman was seen at either 10:00 or 11:00 A.M. (1), as was the woman with chestnut hair (3). Molly's hair is brown (3) and she was seen at either 2:00 or 3:00 P.M. Jackie's hair isn't black (1), so she was seen at either 2:00 or 3:00 P.M. and has blonde hair. So Kate has black hair (2), Jackie was seen at 3:00 P.M., and Molly at 2:00 P.M. The chestnut-haired woman seen at 10:00 A.M. (3) isn't Iona, so Louisa. Iona was thus seen at 11:00 A.M. and has silver hair.

Thus:

Iona - 11:00 A.M. - silver;
Jackie - 3:00 P.M. - blonde;
Kate - 4:00 P.M. - black;
Louisa - 10:00 A.M. - chestnut;
Molly - 2:00 P.M. - brown.

7

The person who wants cocoa and a plain donut (clue 1) isn't Mike (clue 2), Sandie (3), Tony, or Doris (5), so Will. Mike wants coffee but not an iced donut (2), cherry donut (3), or cream donut (4), so a chocolate donut. Sandie wants a cherry donut (3). The person who wants an iced donut isn't Tony (5), so Doris. Thus Tony wants a cream donut. The person who wants cola isn't Sandie or Tony (3), so Doris. Tony doesn't want juice (4), so water. Sandie wants juice.

Thus:

Doris - cola - iced;
Mike - coffee - chocolate;
Sandie - juice - cherry;
Tony - water - cream;
Will - cocoa - plain.

8

Kimberly's surname is Weaver (clue 2) and George's is Crawford (clue 3). Jonathan's isn't Stone (1) or Leigh (3), so Bourne. Caroline's isn't Stone (1), so Leigh. Thus Jessica's surname is Stone. Caroline's slice is either B or D (1), so (3) it's B and George's is thus A. Slice C (2) isn't for Jonathan (Bourne, above). Since Caroline's is B (above), Kimberly's isn't C (2). So Jessica's is C, Kimberly's is D (2), and Jonathan's is E.

Thus:

Slice A - George - Crawford;
Slice B - Caroline - Leigh;
Slice C - Jessica - Stone;
Slice D - Kimberly - Weaver;
Slice E - Jonathan - Bourne.

9

Graham is either 86 or 89 (clue 1), so David is 85 (clue 2), Eddie is either 86 or 89 and Tina's husband is 83 and (by elimination) he's Frank. David is thus married to Amy (1) and Wendy is 87, so Graham is 89. Eddie is 86. Graham's wife is 82 (3), so (by elimination) she's Barbara and Wendy is married to Eddie. Tina (Frank's wife, above) is 81 (4), so Amy is 85.

Thus (his age - her age):

David - Amy - 85 - 85;
Eddie - Wendy - 86 - 87;
Frank - Tina - 83 - 81;
Graham - Barbara - 89 - 82.

10

The gambler who bet on Escapade won $45 (clue 2), so the one who bet on Albatross won $40 (clue 3) and Maggie won $20. Gordon thus won $45, Frank won $50 (1), and the person who bet on Cry Wolf won $25. Diane won either $25 or $40, so (4) the person who bet on Braveheart won $20 (Maggie, above). By elimination, the winner of $50 (Frank, above) bet on Dick's Choice. Diane won $40 (4), so Stan won $25.

Thus:
Diane - Albatross - $40;
Frank - Dick's Choice - $50;
Gordon - Escapade - $45;
Maggie - Braveheart - $20;
Stan - Cry Wolf - $25.

11

Mr. and Mrs. Evans are moving from Iowa (clue 1) and Mr. and Mrs. Cooper are going to Texas (clue 4). The couple moving from California to Florida (3) aren't Mr. and Mrs. Black or Mr. and Mrs. Drake, so Mr. and Mrs. Fisher. By elimination, Mr. and Mrs. Black are moving from Ohio (1) and Mr. and Mrs. Evans are moving to Ohio. Mr. and Mrs. Black are moving to California (2), so Mr. and Mrs. Drake are going to Iowa. Since Mr. and Mrs. Cooper are moving to Texas (4), they aren't moving from Texas (intro), so from Florida. Mr. and Mrs. Drake are moving from Texas.

Thus (from - to):
Mr. and Mrs. Black - Ohio
  - California;
Mr. and Mrs. Cooper - Florida
  - Texas;
Mr. and Mrs. Drake - Texas - Iowa;
Mr. and Mrs. Evans - Iowa - Ohio;
Mr. and Mrs. Fisher - California
  - Florida.

12

The patch made on Monday isn't purple or white (clue 2) or turquoise (clue 3), so green, and (4) isn't patch C, so (1) it's patch A. Patch B is turquoise (3) and the cherry is on either C or D, so isn't on the green patch. Thus the turquoise patch wasn't made on Wednesday (3). The patch made on Wednesday isn't white (2), so purple, and patch A (green, above) has a picture of a plum. The patch made on Saturday is either B or D (1) and hasn't a picture of a cherry (3) or apricot (4), so strawberry. Patch C hasn't a picture of an apricot (4), so a cherry; and wasn't made on Wednesday (4), so on Friday, and Wednesday's patch (purple, above) has an apricot. By elimination, patch D is purple, so patch C is white and patch B has a picture of a strawberry and was made on Saturday.

Thus:
Patch A - green - plum - Monday;
Patch B - turquoise - strawberry
  - Saturday;
Patch C - white - cherry - Friday;
Patch D - purple - apricot
  - Wednesday.

13

The person who typed 21 e-mails isn't Evelyn (clue 1) or Terry (clue 2), so (3) Gloria typed 21 and Justin 20 e-mails. Justin didn't produce 16 or 19 letters (1), so 18 (4) and Terry produced 16 letters. Evelyn produced 18 e-mails (1), so Terry produced 17 e-mails. Terry typed 19 memos (2), so Evelyn produced 17 memos (1) and Gloria typed 17 letters. Evelyn thus typed 19 letters. Justin typed 16 memos (4), so Gloria typed 15 memos.

Thus: (e-mails - letters - memos):
Evelyn - 18 - 19 - 17;
Gloria - 21 - 17 - 15;
Justin - 20 - 18 - 16;
Terry - 17 - 16 - 19.

14

Remember throughout that each child wore his/her own sock on the left foot and a different sock on the right (intro). Benny wore a left black sock (clue 3) and Kenny a left brown sock (clue 4). The child wearing the left blue sock wasn't Lenny or Jenny (1), so Penny. Lenny wore a right blue sock (1), so the child with a left gray sock and right white sock (2) was Jenny. Lenny's left sock was thus white. Benny's right sock wasn't gray (3), so brown. Penny's right sock wasn't gray (5), so black. Kenny wore the gray sock on his right foot.

Thus (left - right):
Benny - black - brown;
Jenny - gray - white;
Kenny - brown - gray;
Lenny - white - blue;
Penny - blue - black.

15

The party on the 20th isn't to celebrate a graduation (clue 1), book launch (clue 2), or birthday (3), so (4) Phil's emigration. Damian's is thus on the 12th (2) and the book launch party is on the 10th. The latter isn't John's (1) or Lester's (3), so Hugh's. The graduation party isn't Damian's or John's (1), so Lester's; thus it's on the 15th and John's is on the 18th. Damian's is the birthday party (3), so the retirement party is John's.

Thus:
Damian - birthday - 12th;
Hugh - book launch - 10th;
John - retirement - 18th;
Lester - graduation - 15th;
Phil - emigration - 20th.

16

The person in seat D (farthest right) isn't Brenda (clue 1), Harry (clue 2), or Viola (3), so is Sean the cooking expert. The person in C isn't Brenda (1) or Viola (3), so Harry. The finance expert is in B (2) and Sean's surname is Moorcroft. Brenda is in B (1) and Harry is the gardening expert. Viola is in A and is an expert in law.

Brenda's surname is Lowe (3). Viola's isn't Wallis (4), so Stevenson. Harry's surname is Wallis.

Thus:

Person A - Viola - Stevenson - law;
Person B - Brenda - Lowe - finance;
Person C - Harry - Wallis - gardening;
Person D - Sean - Moorcroft - cooking.

17

Photo D (farthest right) isn't of Uncle Joseph or Aunt Jane (clue 1) or Uncle David (clue 2), so Aunt Eliza. Picture C was taken in April (3), so (2) D was taken in August. Photo A was taken in June (4), so photo B in October. Photo A wasn't taken in 2001 (1), 1999, (2) or 2003 (4), so 1997. B wasn't taken in 2001 (1) or 2003 (5), so 1999. Uncle David is the subject of photo A (2). The 2001 photo isn't of Uncle Joseph or Aunt Jane (1), so Aunt Eliza (D, above), thus photo C was taken in 2003. The photo of Aunt Jane isn't C (3), so B. C is of Uncle Joseph.

Thus:

Photo A - Uncle David - June - 1997;
Photo B - Aunt Jane - October - 1999;
Photo C - Uncle Joseph - April - 2003;
Photo D - Aunt Eliza - August - 2001.

18

The sage was eaten at 12:30 P.M. (clue 3), so the pigs weren't in the yard at 11:00 A.M. (clue 2). The animals found at 11:00 A.M. weren't cows (1) or sheep (4), so chickens. The cows were thus found at 12:30 P.M. (1), so the sheep at 2:00 P.M. (4), thus the pigs at 9:30 A.M. There were 5 cows (3), so 6 chickens (1). The chickens were eating marigolds (2). The pigs weren't eating parsley (2), so nasturtiums. The sheep were eating parsley. There weren't 4 pigs (5), so 3. There were 4 sheep.

Thus:

Chickens - 11:00 A.M. - 6 - marigolds;
Cows - 12:30 P.M. - 5 - sage;
Pigs - 9:30 A.M. - 3 - nasturtiums;
Sheep - 2:00 P.M. - 4 - parsley.

19

Remember throughout that each picture is made up of parts of three different pictures (intro). Nora's aunt's body is in the same picture as her sister's legs (clue 1) and her sister's body is with her grandpa's head (clue 3). Nora's uncle's legs and cousin's head (2) are thus with her grandpa's body. By elimination, her aunt's body and sister's legs are with her uncle's head. Her grandpa's legs aren't with her sister's head (4), so they're with her aunt's head; not with her uncle's body (5), so her cousin's body. Her sister's head isn't with her aunt's legs (1), so her cousin's. Her aunt's legs are in the same picture as her grandpa's head.

Thus (head - body - legs):
Aunt - cousin - grandpa;
Cousin - grandpa - uncle;
Grandpa - sister - aunt;
Sister - uncle - cousin;
Uncle - aunt - sister.

20

The woman who ran in lane 1 isn't Charlotte (clue 2), Doreen (clue 3), or Frances (4), so Edith was in lane 1, the woman in lilac was in lane 2 (1), and the woman in lane 3 came in second. Edith wasn't in pink (4), so the woman in lane 3 wore pink and Frances ran in lane 4. Frances wasn't first (2) or third (4), so fourth. Her tracksuit wasn't turquoise (3), so beige, and (by elimination) Edith's was turquoise. Edith was thus first (3) and Doreen, second. By elimination, Charlotte was third and ran in lane 2.

Thus:
Lane 1 - Edith - first - turquoise;
Lane 2 - Charlotte - third - lilac;
Lane 3 - Doreen - second - pink;
Lane 4 - Frances - fourth - beige.

21

From the listed ages (grid) the only possible difference of four years is 97 (his age) and 93 (her age), so Norman is 97 and his wife is 93 (clue 2). No woman is 97 (grid), so Maud's

husband isn't 94 (clue 3), nor can he be 97 or 98. Thus Maud's husband is 93, Frances is 96 (3), and Maud is 91. Naomi is married to Harold (4), so Norman's wife (aged 93, above) is Clarice. By elimination, Naomi is 99. Edgar's wife is 96 (1), so she's Frances and Maud is married to Philip. Edgar is 94 (1), so Harold is 98.

Thus (his age - her age):
Edgar - Frances - 94 - 96;
Harold - Naomi - 98 - 99;
Norman - Clarice - 97 - 93;
Philip - Maud - 93 - 91.

22

The St. Luke's pupil's favorite subject is drama (clue 1) and Olga's is science (clue 3). Peter went to Woodford School (4) and his favorite is neither music nor art, so English. Caroline's is neither music nor drama (5), so art. Hal's isn't music (2), so drama, and John's favorite is music. By elimination, the boy (3) who went to Fortcliff is John. The former High Hill pupil isn't Caroline (5), so Olga. Caroline attended Portwood School.

Thus:
Caroline - Portwood - art;
Hal - St Luke's - drama;
John - Fortcliff - music;
Olga - High Hill - science;
Peter - Woodford - English.

23

Drink E (farthest right) isn't called Bee's Sting or Dynamighty (clue 1), Eve's Folly (clue 2), or Cornucopia (3), so Abe's Antidote. Drink A (farthest left) isn't Eve's Folly (2) or Cornucopia (3), so A is a Bee's Sting (1) and B is called Dynamighty. Eve's Folly is green (2). Drink A isn't blue (1), brown, or turquoise (3), so pink. Abe's Antidote (E, above) isn't brown (3). Nor is Cornucopia brown (3), so the brown drink is Dynamighty. Drink C is thus Cornucopia (3), so Eve's Folly is D. Drink E is turquoise (3), so C is blue.

Thus:

Drink A - Bee's Sting - pink;
Drink B - Dynamighty - brown;
Drink C - Cornucopia - blue;
Drink D - Eve's Folly - green;
Drink E - Abe's Antidote - turquoise.

24

The door of No. 3 isn't green (clue 1), red or cream (clue 2), or black (3), so blue. Jimmy lives at No. 4 (1), so Deborah lives at No. 3 (3) and Martin, at No. 2. Martin's door isn't green (1), red, or black (3), so cream. The house with the red door has a number more than two higher than that of the one with the cream door (2), so the door of No. 5 is red. Pam lives at No. 1 (4) and Bill, at No. 5. Pam's door isn't red or black (4), so green. Thus Bill lives at No. 5, Pam lives at No. 1, and Jimmy's door is black.

Thus:

No. 1 - Pam - green;
No. 2 - Martin - cream;
No. 3 - Deborah - blue;
No. 4 - Jimmy - black;
No. 5 - Bill - red.

25

The conference with 265 delegates wasn't entitled "Broad Outlook" (clue 1), "Clients Count" (clue 3), "New Horizons" (4), or "Fast Forward" (5), so "Great Ideas." Its delegates weren't from Illinois (2), so there weren't 283 at the "Broad Outlook" conference. The one with 283 delegates wasn't entitled "New Horizons" (4) or "Fast Forward" (5), so "Clients Count." Thus the "Great Ideas" delegates were from Texas (3). The conference with 292 delegates wasn't entitled "New Horizons" (4) or "Fast Forward" (5), so "Broad Outlook." The "Clients Count" conference attendees were from Illinois (1). The "Broad Outlook" conference delegates were from Kansas (4) and there were 301 delegates at the "New Horizons" conference; so the "Fast Forward" conference had 319 attendees. The "New Horizons" conference delegates came from Florida (2), so the "Fast Forward" delegates were from Ohio.

Thus:

"Broad Outlook" - 292 - Kansas;
"Clients Count" - 283 - Illinois;
"Fast Forward" - 319 - Ohio;
"Great Ideas" - 265 - Texas;
"New Horizons" - 301 - Florida.

26

Remember throughout that each family is made up of people whose names begin with four different letters (intro). Chrissie and her son Liam (clue 2) are thus unrelated to Charles or Larry, Caroline or Leonie. Chrissie's daughter isn't Debbie (clue 2), so Angelica, thus Chrissie's husband isn't Alan, so Dicky. Alan's wife isn't Dawn (1), so (by elimination) she's Lily, and Leonie is Charles's daughter. Charles isn't married to Dawn (1), so Anne, thus their son is Damian. By elimination, Aidan is Larry's son and Alan's son is Colin, so Alan's daughter is Debbie and Larry's daughter is Carolyn.

Thus:

Alan - Lily - Colin - Debbie;
Charles - Anne - Damian - Leonie;
Dicky - Chrissie - Liam - Angelica;
Larry - Dawn - Aidan - Carolyn.

27

Katie's puppet is called Clacker (clue 3). Anne owns the clown puppet (clue 4). So the girl (1) who owns Arabella the ballet dancer is Louisa. The girl (1) who owns the pixie puppet is thus Katie. Dean owns the mule puppet (3), so the dragon named Snort (2) belongs to Benjamin. Anne's puppet isn't called Walpole (4), so Mosie. Dean's puppet is Walpole.

Thus:

Anne - clown - Mosie;
Benjamin - dragon - Snort;
Dean - mule - Walpole;
Katie - pixie - Clacker;
Louisa - ballet dancer - Arabella.

28

No one delivered 13 parcels (grid). The courier who traveled 96 miles didn't deliver 16 (clue 3) or 12 parcels (clue 4), so 15 (1) and David delivered 14. Thus Laura delivered 16 (5) and David traveled 88 miles. The courier who delivered 12 parcels isn't Carl (2) or Richard (4), so Sandra. She traveled six more miles than Laura (3) and four fewer than Richard (4), so Sandra traveled 92 miles, Laura 86 and Richard 96. Richard delivered 15 parcels (1) and Carl delivered 11 (2). Carl traveled 98 miles.

Thus:

Carl - 11 parcels - 98 miles;
David - 14 parcels - 88 miles;
Laura - 16 parcels - 86 miles;
Richard - 15 parcels - 96 miles;
Sandra - 12 parcels - 92 miles.

29

The books were bought in Tampa (clue 1). Clothing wasn't bought in Sarasota (clue 2) or Miami (3), so Orlando. Porcelain wasn't bought in Sarasota (2), so Miami; thus paintings were bought in Sarasota. The Sarasota fair was in the summer (2). The Miami fair was later than that in Orlando (3), which wasn't in the spring (1), so the spring fair was in Tampa; the autumn fair in Orlando, and the winter fair, in Miami. Hal spent $550 in Miami (3), so $790 in Sarasota (2) and $670 in Tampa. The $910 was spent in Orlando.

Thus:

Spring - Tampa - books - $670;
Summer - Sarasota - paintings - $790;
Autumn - Orlando - clothing - $910;
Winter - Miami - porcelain - $550.

30

Felicity's prediction concerned marriage (clue 3) and Mark's, a trip abroad. The prediction of a career change came from reading tea leaves (clue 1) and wasn't given to Christopher, so to Sharon. Christopher's prediction was thus of an inheritance and (1) will happen next month. Mark's palm was read (3). The crystal ball prediction was given for next Tuesday (2), so Christopher's was by tarot cards and Felicity's, by crystal ball. Thus Mark's prediction will happen next Friday (3) and Sharon's tomorrow.

Thus:

Christopher - inheritance - tarot cards - next month;
Felicity - marriage - crystal ball - next Tuesday;
Mark - trip abroad - palm reading - next Friday;
Sharon - career change - tea leaves - tomorrow.

31

Shane donated to the charity for birds (clue 1) and Stan to the children's charity (clue 4). The charity for animals didn't receive a donation from Sally (2), so Sadie. Sally gave to the war widows' charity. She bought a sticker from Faith (2). The shopper who gave $5 to Hope (3) isn't Sadie or Stan (4), so Shane. The one who gave $4 to Verity (5) isn't Stan (4), so Sadie. Thus Stan gave $3 (4) and (by elimination) he bought a sticker from Honor. Sally donated $2.

Thus:

Sadie - animals - $4 - Verity;
Sally - war widows - $2 - Faith;
Shane - birds - $5 - Hope;
Stan - children - $3 - Honor.

32

The woman who starred in *Old Habits* doesn't host *Good Evening* (clue 2), *Ask a Friend*, or *Why Not?* (clue 3), so *Talk to Me*. She isn't Cathy (1), Norma, or Patsy (2), so Madeleine. Madeleine isn't Ms. Grant or Ms. Fisher (1), or Ms. Donelly (3), so Ms. Jones. The host of *Good Evening* isn't Norma or Patsy (2), so Cathy. She didn't star in *Stephanie* (1), so either *Cloud Nine* or *Joking Apart*, thus (4) Cathy isn't Ms. Fisher. Nor is she Ms. Grant (1), so Ms. Donelly. Patsy isn't Ms. Fisher (2), so Ms. Grant and Norma is Ms. Fisher. Norma didn't star in *Cloud Nine* or *Joking Apart* (4), so *Stephanie*. The host of *Ask a Friend* isn't Norma (3), so Patsy. Norma thus hosts *Why Not?* Patsy didn't star in *Joking Apart* (4), so *Cloud Nine*. The former star of *Joking Apart* is Cathy.

Thus:

Cathy - Donelly - *Joking Apart* - *Good Evening*;

Madeleine - Jones - *Old Habits* - *Talk to Me*;

Norma - Fisher - *Stephanie* - *Why Not?*;

Patsy - Grant - *Cloud Nine* - *Ask a Friend*.

33

The 750-piece jigsaw picture isn't the city skyline (clue 1), mountains, horses, or harbor (clue 2), so the flowers. The 1,000-piece jigsaw picture isn't the city skyline (1), harbor, or horses (2), so mountains. It's being done by Deborah (2), so Harold's puzzle has 750 pieces (1) and the city skyline puzzle has 1,500. Juan's puzzle isn't the city skyline or horses (1), so the harbor. Kathleen's puzzle has more pieces than Peter's (3), so Peter's is the city skyline puzzle and Kathleen's is of horses. Kathleen's hasn't 3,000 pieces (3), so 2,000. The 3,000-piece jigsaw is Juan's.

Thus:

City skyline - Peter - 1,500 pieces;

Flowers - Harold - 750 pieces;

Harbor - Juan - 3,000 pieces;

Horses - Kathleen - 2,000 pieces;

Mountains - Deborah - 1,000 pieces.

34

Miss Arran was a bank clerk (clue 2) and Ms. Foster now teaches geography (clue 3). The former accountant who now teaches history (1) isn't Mr. Cole or Mrs. Doyle, so Mr. Gold. Miss Arran doesn't teach mathematics or music (2), so biology. Ms. Foster wasn't formerly a tailor or a mechanic (3), so a store manager. Mr. Cole doesn't teach music (4), so mathematics. Thus he wasn't formerly a mechanic (5), so a tailor. Mrs. Doyle is thus the former mechanic who now teaches music.

Thus:

Miss Arran - bank clerk - biology;

Mr. Cole - tailor - mathematics;

Mrs. Doyle - mechanic - music;

Ms. Foster - store manager - geography;

Mr. Gold - accountant - history.

35

The person surnamed Edmonton has seat D (clue 4), so (clue 1) Edmonton works in Finance, the person surnamed Collins has seat C and David with his back to the engine sits in B. David is opposite Edmonton (1), thus David's surname isn't Davis (2), so Bourne. Davis thus has seat A. So Collins works in Sales (2) and Frank has D. Edward has C (3), so George has A. The Marketing employee isn't in A (3), so B. The Personnel employee has seat A.

Thus:

Seat A - George - Davis - Personnel;
Seat B - David - Bourne - Marketing;
Seat C - Edward - Collins - Sales;
Seat D - Frank - Edmonton - Finance.

36

The person who bought 7 apples (fewest) isn't Ruth (clue 1), George (clue 2), Steve (3), or Kenny (4), so Barbara, and (3) Steve bought 9 apples. Thus Kenny bought 10 apples (1) and Ruth bought 11. By elimination, George bought 8 apples. Kenny bought 8 pears (4). The person who bought 12 pears (most) isn't Ruth (1), Steve (2), or Barbara (3), so George. Barbara bought 11 pears (3), so Steve bought 10 (2). Ruth bought 9 pears.

Thus:

Barbara - 7 apples - 11 pears;
George - 8 apples - 12 pears;
Kenny - 10 apples - 8 pears;
Ruth - 11 apples - 9 pears;
Steve - 9 apples - 10 pears.

37

The woman who bought the $60 dress first isn't Beth (clue 1), Carly (clue 2), Fran, or Donna (3), so Edina. The one who bought the $30 dress second isn't Beth (1), Carly (2), Edina, or Donna (3), so Fran. Beth's second purchase cost either $55 or $60 (clue 1), as did Donna's (3), so Carly's second was $45 and her first was $40. Thus Edina's second was $40 and Donna's second was $55 (3). Beth's second was thus $60, so (1) her first was $50. Donna ($55 on her second, above) didn't spend $55 on her first (intro), so $45. Fran spent $55 on her first purchase.

Thus (first - second):

Beth - $50 - $60;
Carly - $40 - $45;
Donna - $45 - $55;
Edina - $60 - $40;
Fran - $55 - $30.

38

Cushion E was made in April (clue 3), so cushion D was made in either February or June (clue 1), as was cushion B (2). The cat isn't on E (1) and neither the cat nor the birds are on D. The birds aren't on B (2), so the birds are on C (1) and the cat is on B. C was thus made in October (1) and D in June. By elimination, A was made August and B was made in February. The sunflowers are on E (2). The roses aren't on D (1), so A. D has a picture of an apple tree.

Thus:

Cushion A - August - roses;
Cushion B - February - cat;
Cushion C - October - birds;
Cushion D - June - apple tree;
Cushion E - April - sunflowers.

39

The baby born on Monday isn't Bella or Ruth (clue 1), Christine or Alan (clue 3), so Perry. The one born on Tuesday isn't Bella or Ruth (1), so Christine (3), and Alan was born on Wednesday. Bella was thus born on Thursday (1) and Ruth, on Friday. Christine's mother is Leslie (1) and Perry's mother is Lucy (3). Lynne's daughter (2) isn't Ruth (born on Friday, above), so Bella, and Liz's child is Ruth. Alan's mother is Laura.

Thus:

Laura - Alan - Wednesday;
Leslie - Christine - Tuesday;
Liz - Ruth - Friday;
Lucy - Perry - Monday;
Lynne - Bella - Thursday.

40

The blue lamp was bought on Wednesday (clue 4) and lamp E on Thursday. The pink lamp wasn't bought on Friday (clue 2), so D was bought on either Friday or Saturday (3), the pink lamp was bought on Thursday and the orange lamp, on Tuesday. Lamp D was thus bought on Friday (2) and isn't yellow, so beige. The yellow lamp was bought on Saturday. Lamp A was bought on Wednesday (1) and the orange lamp is C (next to and left of beige), so B is yellow.

Thus:

Tuesday - lamp C - orange;
Wednesday - lamp A - blue;
Thursday - lamp E - pink;
Friday - lamp D - beige;
Saturday - lamp B - yellow.

41

Shirley's favorite is *News Review* (clue 2) and James's is *Natural World* (clue 3). *Laughter Time* is on Tuesdays and isn't the favorite of Michelle (1) or Jose (4), so Timothy. Jose's favorite on Saturdays (4) isn't *Sports World* (3), so *World Events*. Michelle thus watches *Sports World*. *Sports World* is broadcast on Thursdays and *Natural World* on Fridays (3), so Shirley's favorite is on Mondays.

Thus:

James - *Natural World* - Fridays;
Jose - *World Events* - Saturdays;
Michelle - *Sports World* - Thursdays;
Shirley - *News Review* - Mondays;
Timothy - *Laughter Time* - Tuesdays.

42

The ride on which a child had 7 (most) turns isn't the big dipper (clue 1), pirate boat, or roller coaster (clue 2), or bumper cars (3), so the merry-go-round. Louis' favorite is the bumper cars (3). The child who had 3 (fewest) turns isn't Carole (1), Michael (2), Louis, or Sally (3), so Freddie, whose favorite isn't the big dipper (1) or roller coaster (2), so pirate boat. Thus the child whose favorite is the roller coaster went on 5 times (2) and Michael had either 6 or 7 turns. Sally's favorite isn't the merry-go-round (3), so (by elimination) Louis went on the bumper cars 4 times, Sally went on the roller coaster 5 times, and one child had 6 turns on the big dipper. The latter isn't Carole (1), so Michael. Carole thus went 7 times on the merry-go-round.

Thus:
Carole - merry-go-round - 7 times;
Freddie - pirate boat - 3 times;
Louis - bumper cars - 4 times;
Michael - big dipper - 6 times;
Sally - roller coaster - 5 times.

43

Lucy's 5th visit wasn't to the drugstore (clue 1), supermarket (clue 2), clothes store, or shoe shop (3), so the bookshop, where (4) she saw Carol. Virginia wasn't in the supermarket (2), nor was she in the clothes store or shoe shop (3), so the drugstore. The clothes store was visited directly before the shoe shop, which was visited directly before the drugstore (3), which was visited directly before the shop in which Lucy saw Donna (1), so the clothes store was 1st, shoe shop 2nd, drugstore 3rd, and Donna was seen in the 4th shop, which was thus the supermarket. Ann wasn't in the shoe shop (4), so she was in the clothes store and Karen was in the shoe shop.

Thus:
Bookshop - 5th - Carol;
Clothes store - 1st - Ann;
Drugstore - 3rd - Virginia;
Shoe shop - 2nd - Karen;
Supermarket - 4th - Donna.

44

Remember throughout that every man gave three items containing different types of gemstones (intro). Kurt gave a sapphire necklace (clue 3), thus not a sapphire bracelet or sapphire ring. The man who gave a ruby ring and emerald necklace (clue 2) didn't give a sapphire bracelet, so a diamond bracelet. These weren't gifts from Hal or Maurice (1), so Robert. Hal thus gave an emerald ring (1) and Maurice gave the emerald bracelet. By elimination, Kurt gave the ruby bracelet and diamond ring, and Hal gave the sapphire bracelet and emerald ring. Hal's necklace didn't have diamonds (1), so rubies. Maurice gave the necklace of diamonds.

Thus (bracelet - necklace - ring):
Hal - sapphires - rubies - emeralds;
Kurt - rubies - sapphires - diamonds;
Maurice - emeralds - diamonds - sapphires;
Robert - diamonds - emeralds - rubies.

45

Sarah's four-letter word was either "Meat" or "Pale" (clue 4), so Andrea is the woman (clue 1) who made both "Empty" and "Mile." Tim didn't make "Plate" (3). The player who made both "Item" and "Plate" isn't George (2), so Will. The one who made "Emit" thus isn't Tim (3), so George. George's four-letter word started with "E," so (5) his five-letter word was "Metal." Sarah's wasn't "Imply" (4), so "Ample" and her four-letter word was "Pale." Tim's words were "Meat" and "Imply."

Thus:

Andrea - Mile - Empty;
George - Emit - Metal;
Sarah - Pale - Ample;
Tim - Meat - Imply;
Will - Item - Plate.

46

Either Edgar lives at No. 5 and Sue is at No. 3 (clue 1) or Edgar lives at No. 3 and Sue at No. 1. In other words, either Edgar or Sue lives at No. 3. Wendy is at either No. 2 or No. 4 (clue 1), so Rose and Henry (2) live at No. 5, Tanya lives at No. 3, Edgar lives at No. 3 (1), Sue is at No. 1 and Wendy is at No. 2. By elimination, Vera lives at No. 4. Danny is at No. 1 (3), and Gordon at No. 2, so Vera is Ivan's wife.

Thus:

Danny - Sue - No. 1;
Edgar - Tanya - No. 3;
Gordon - Wendy - No. 2;
Henry - Rose - No. 5;
Ivan - Vera - No. 4.

47

The card sent to Amy, who doesn't live in Rome or Tokyo (clue 2), was posted on either Thursday or Friday. The card sent to Johannesburg was posted on either Monday or Tuesday (clue 1), so wasn't addressed to Amy. Thus Amy lives in Paris. Aileen's card was also posted on either Thursday or Friday (1) and the card sent to Rome was posted on either Monday or Tuesday (2), so (by elimination) Aileen lives in Tokyo. Miriam sent a card to Aster (3) who doesn't live in Rome, so Johannesburg. Alison lives in Rome; her card wasn't from Madge (2) and Madge didn't post a card to Amy. So Madge sent a card to Aileen. Madge's card wasn't posted on Friday (2), so on Thursday (1) and the one to Johannesburg was posted on Monday. The card to Rome was posted on Tuesday (2), so (by elimination) Muriel posted a card on Friday, and Megan on Tuesday.

Thus:

Madge - Thursday - Aileen - Tokyo;
Megan - Tuesday - Alison - Rome;
Miriam - Monday - Aster
   - Johannesburg;
Muriel - Friday - Amy - Paris.

48

Jean's boyfriend is Gerald (clue 1), and Cheryl's boyfriend is Keith (clue 3). Justin's girlfriend isn't Gloria or Sarah (2), so Evelyn. Terry's class is either Monday or Tuesday (1), so his girlfriend isn't Gloria (2). Thus Gloria's boyfriend is Sam and Sarah's is Terry. The woman who dances on Friday isn't Jean or Sarah (1), Gloria (2), or Cheryl (3), so Evelyn. Jean dances on Wednesday (1) and Sarah on Tuesday, so Gloria dances on Thursday (2). Cheryl dances on Monday.

Thus:

Cheryl - Keith - Monday;
Evelyn - Justin - Friday;
Gloria - Sam - Thursday;
Jean - Gerald - Wednesday;
Sarah - Terry - Tuesday.

49

The child whose preferred second ingredient is salmon is either 6 or 8 years old (clue 1), as is the child who likes both cheese and honey (clue 2). Thus the child who likes marmalade is 5 (1) and Mary is 4 years old. Carl is 6 (2) and the child who likes honey and cheese is 8, so (1) the one who likes salmon is 6. Annie is 5 (3) and the child who likes peanut butter is 6. By elimination, William is 8 and Mary's first choice of ingredient is plum jam. Mary's second choice of ingredient isn't cucumber (4), so egg. Annie's is cucumber.

Thus (first - second):

Annie - 5 - marmalade - cucumber;
Carl - 6 - peanut butter - salmon;
Mary - 4 - plum jam - egg;
William - 8 - honey - cheese.

50

Elizabeth wanted a kite (clue 2) and Marianne, a doll (clue 4). Suzie did the dusting (4), thus didn't want the ball (cleaning car, 1) or spinning top (shopping, 3), so the jump rope. The girl who wanted a spinning top and did the shopping isn't Dina (3), so Katie. By elimination, the one who wanted a ball and cleaned the car (1) is Dina. Elizabeth didn't do the vacuuming (2), so gardening, and Marianne did the vacuuming.

Thus:

Dina - ball - cleaning car;
Elizabeth - kite - gardening;
Katie - spinning top - shopping;
Marianne - doll - vacuuming;
Suzie - jump rope - dusting.

51

The woman who visits on Mondays isn't Pam (clue 1), Vera or Joanne (clue 2), or Mary (3), so Holly. Vera does the ironing (2). The washing is done on either Mondays or Tuesdays (1), so not by Joanne (2) or Mary. The washing isn't done by Pam (1), so by Holly. The woman who visits on Fridays isn't Pam (1) or Vera (2), so (3) Joanne visits on Thursdays and Mary on Fridays. The cooking isn't done by Joanne or Mary (2), so Pam. Pam visits on Tuesdays (1), so Vera on Wednesdays. The cleaning is done on Thursdays (1), so the shopping on Fridays.

Thus:

Mondays - Holly - washing;
Tuesdays - Pam - cooking;
Wednesdays - Vera - ironing;
Thursdays - Joanne - cleaning;
Fridays - Mary - shopping.

52

The game in Chicago lasted for 50 minutes (clue 4), so the game in Los Angeles lasted for 60 minutes (clue 2) and the 75-minute game was against Kris King. The game against Kris King won Peter $450 (3), so the match in Dallas won him $600 (2). By elimination, the match against Kris King was in New York and the game in Dallas lasted 65 minutes. Peter didn't win $400 in Chicago (4), so $300 in Chicago and $400 in Los Angeles. Peter didn't win $300 from his match against Ray Rook (5), so didn't play him in Chicago (50 minutes, above). Thus he played Ray Rook for 65 minutes (5). The game in Chicago was thus against Colin Castle (1) and the match against Kurt Knight was in Los Angeles.

Thus:

Chicago - Colin Castle - 50 minutes - $300;
Dallas - Ray Rook - 65 minutes - $600;
Los Angeles - Kurt Knight - 60 minutes - $400;
New York - Kris King - 75 minutes - $450.

53

The man away on Friday wasn't Adam or Chris (clue 1), Eugene (clue 3) or Ben (4), so Dean. Eugene was away on Thursday (3) due to a stomach ache, so the man with a sick child was away on Friday (1), Adam was away on Wednesday, and Chris on Tuesday. Thus Ben was away on Monday. Ben went to a funeral (2). Adam didn't have a migraine (5), so a car problem. Chris had a migraine.

Thus:

Adam - Wednesday - car problem;
Ben - Monday - funeral;
Chris - Tuesday - migraine;
Dean - Friday - sick child;
Eugene - Thursday - stomach ache.

54

No class takes place on Thursdays (grid). The 2:30 P.M. classes are on Wednesdays (clue 3), so the aerobics classes at either 11:00 A.M. or 11:30 A.M. (clue 2) are on Fridays and Lauren goes to yoga with Dawn on Wednesdays. Babs thus goes to the classes which start at 3:00 P.M. (1).

The aerobics classes (Fridays, above) aren't at 11:00 A.M. (4), so 11:30 A.M. The 11:00 A.M. classes aren't swimming (4), so trampoline. Swimming is thus at 3:00 P.M. Trampoline classes are on Mondays (4) and swimming classes on Tuesdays. Erica doesn't go to trampoline sessions (5), so she goes to aerobics classes and Cheryl to trampoline sessions.

Thus:

Aerobics - 11:30 A.M. - Fridays
  - Erica;
Swimming - 3:00 P.M. - Tuesdays
  - Babs;
Trampoline - 11:00 A.M. - Mondays
  - Cheryl;
Yoga - 2:30 P.M. - Wednesdays
  - Dawn.

55

Nero won fourth prize (clue 3), so Nelson won third (clue 1), Mr. Jones's dog won first, and Miss Neame's won either fourth or fifth prize. Hannibal, who belongs to Mrs. Kent (2), was placed second; Mr. O'Connor's dog is Nero; and Brutus won first prize. Third prize thus went to the dog owned by Mr. Morris and fifth prize to Samson, who belongs to Miss Neame.

Thus:

First prize - Brutus - Mr. Jones;
Second prize - Hannibal - Mrs. Kent;
Third prize - Nelson - Mr. Morris;
Fourth prize - Nero - Mr. O'Connor;
Fifth prize - Samson - Miss Neame.

56

No one spent $35 on beer (grid). Either the person who spent $40 on wine spent $45 on beer and Clarice Fletcher spent $40 on beer (clue 2) or the person who spent $40 on wine spent $50 on beer and Clarice Fletcher spent $45 on beer. In other words, the person who spent $45 on beer is either Clarice Fletcher or the shopper who spent $40 on wine. Thus the one surnamed Cooper didn't spend $45 on beer (clue 1). The person surnamed Lang spent $35 on wine (3), so Cooper spent $40 on beer and $45 on wine (1). Clarice Fletcher spent $50 on wine (2), so the person surnamed Vale spent $40 on wine and $50 on beer, Clarice spent $45 on beer, and Lang spent $30. Jade's surname is Cooper (3). Lang's total bill was $65 and Vale's was $90, so Anthony is Vale (4) and Nigel's surname is Lang.

Thus (beer - wine):

Anthony - Vale - $50 - $40;
Clarice - Fletcher - $45 - $50;
Jade - Cooper - $40 - $45;
Nigel - Lang - $30 - $35.

57

The person surnamed Dawson is a man ("Mr.," clue 2), so isn't Jenny or Judy. Sammy's owner is Jenny, whose surname isn't Williams or Brown (clue 4), so Smith. Judy lives at either No. 3 or No. 4 (1), thus isn't surnamed Williams (3), so Brown. Since Williams lives at No. 1 (3), Mr. Dawson lives at

No. 3 (2). Thus Judy (not Mr. Dawson) lives at No. 4 (above). By elimination, Jenny lives at No. 2, so (1) Bonzo is at No. 1. Thus Sammy lives at No. 2, Fifi lives at No. 4 (2) and Wolfie at No. 3. Joseph isn't at No. 3 (5), so No. 1. James lives at No. 3.

Thus:
No. 1 - Bonzo - Joseph - Williams;
No. 2 - Sammy - Jenny - Smith;
No. 3 - Wolfie - James - Dawson;
No. 4 - Fifi - Judy - Brown.

58

The flowers in the pot bought in August aren't white (clue 1), red or orange (clue 2), or blue (3), so yellow, and (1) the one with white flowers was bought in May. Thus the pot with red flowers was bought in February (2) and the one with orange flowers was bought in April. So the pot with blue flowers was bought in July. Pot C was bought in August (3), so (2) the one with red flowers is either A or B. February's pot has red flowers (above), so (1) it's A and pot B has white flowers. D was bought in April (4) and E in July.

Thus:
Pot A - February - red;
Pot B - May - white;
Pot C - August - yellow;
Pot D - April - orange;
Pot E - July - blue.

59

No animal has been owned for 12 months (grid). The gerbil has been owned for either 8 or 10 months (clue 1), as has the tortoise (clue 2), so Gemma the cat has been with Josie for 14 months (3) and the dog, for 16 months. By elimination, the rabbit has been with Josie for 6 months. Clover is the dog (1) and the gerbil has been with Josie for 10 months. Thus the tortoise has been with Josie for 8 months (2), Marty has been with her for 6 months, and Freddie, for 10 months. The tortoise is called Topsy.

Thus:
Clover - dog - 16 months;
Freddie - gerbil - 10 months;
Gemma - cat - 14 months;
Marty - rabbit - 6 months;
Topsy - tortoise - 8 months.

60

John took either 9 or 10 bottles (clue 1), as did Lenny (clue 2), so Karen and Maureen took 7 and/or 8 bottles. Thus Karen took 8 bottles and 8 papers (4) and Maureen took 7 bottles. Lenny took 9 bottles (2). John took 10 bottles and 9 papers (1). Lenny took 11 cans (3), so John took 10 cans (1) and Maureen, 12 cans. Thus Karen took 13 cans, so (5) Maureen took 10 papers. Lenny took 11 papers.

Thus (bottles - cans - papers):
John - 10 - 10 - 9;
Karen 8 - 13 - 8;
Lenny - 9 - 11 - 11;
Maureen - 7 - 12 - 10.

61

No event starts at 7:00 P.M. (grid). Bridge club starts at 7:15 P.M. (clue 3). Bowling is on Thursday (clue 2), so doesn't start at 8:00 P.M. (1). Thus the bowling starts at 7:45 P.M. (2) and the dinner party at 7:30 P.M. The theater trip isn't at 8:00 P.M. (1), so 6:45 P.M. The fashion show starts at 8:00 P.M. Friday's event isn't the fashion show (1), bridge club, or dinner party (3), so the theater trip. The fashion show is on Wednesday (1). The bridge club is on Monday (3) and the dinner party on Tuesday.

Thus:

Bowling - 7:45 P.M. - Thursday;
Bridge club - 7:15 P.M. - Monday.
Dinner party - 7:30 P.M. - Tuesday;
Fashion show - 8:00 P.M.
    - Wednesday;
Theater trip - 6:45 P.M. - Friday.

62

Remember throughout that each "new" picture contains pieces of three "old" ones (intro). The head of the rhinoceros and elephant's legs are not with the body of the giraffe (clue 1) or dog (with the legs of the rhinoceros, clue 4), so they're with the cat's body. The elephant's head hasn't the body of the giraffe (2) or dog (4), so rhinoceros. They're not with the legs of the giraffe (2) or cat (3), so dog. The cat's legs aren't with the giraffe's head (3), so the dog's. By elimination, the giraffe's legs are with the cat's head. The rhinoceros's legs and dog's body (4) are with the giraffe's head. Thus the cat's head and (above) giraffe's legs are with the elephant's body, and the giraffe's body is with the dog's head.

Thus (head - body - legs):

Cat - elephant - giraffe;
Dog - giraffe - cat;
Elephant - rhinoceros - dog;
Giraffe - dog - rhinoceros;
Rhinoceros - cat - elephant.

63

The Chipp chair was made in 1823 (clue 3), so the Whyte chair was made in 1827 (clue 1) and the Heppel chair in 1819. Thus the Dale chair was made in 1815. The Chipp chair is next to and right of the Heppel chair (3), so the Chipp chair is oak (1). The beech chair wasn't made in 1827 (2), so isn't the Whyte chair. Nor was it made by Heppel (2). So Dale made the beech chair. The Heppel chair (1819, above) is walnut (2), so the Whyte chair is mahogany. The Heppel chair isn't B (2), so C (1), and the Chipp chair is D. Chair A wasn't made by Dale (4), so Whyte. Dale made chair B.

Thus:

Chair A - Whyte - 1827
    - mahogany;
Chair B - Dale - 1815 - beech;
Chair C - Heppel - 1819 - walnut;
Chair D - Chipp - 1823 - oak.

SOLUTIONS

64

Katie dressed as a witch (clue 1). The person dressed as a ghost wasn't Laura or Joe (clue 2) and didn't arrive first, so (3) wasn't Martin. Thus Paul dressed as a ghost. Martin arrived 1st (3). The person who arrived 2nd wasn't Katie (1), Laura, or Paul (2), so Joe. The one who arrived 5th wasn't Katie or Paul (1), so Laura. Katie was 4th (1) and Paul was 3rd. Laura dressed as a mummy (1). Martin didn't dress as a vampire (3), so a skeleton. Joe wore the vampire costume.

Thus:

Joe - vampire - 2nd;
Katie - witch - 4th;
Laura - mummy - 5th;
Martin - skeleton - 1st;
Paul - ghost - 3rd.

65

Either the man who went to the theater left at 7:30 and the one who went to the nightclub left at 7:15 (clue 2), or the man who went to the theater left at 7:15 and the one who went to the nightclub left at 7:00. In other words, the man who left at 7:15 went to either the theater or the nightclub. Kenny, who went to the restaurant, didn't leave at 7:00 (clue 3), or 7:40 (4), so 7:30. Thus the man who went to the theater left at 7:15 (above), the one who went to the nightclub left at 7:00 (2), and the one who went to the cinema left at 7:40. Denny who left earlier than Kenny (3) didn't go to

the nightclub, so Denny left at 7:15. Benny didn't leave at 7:00 (1), so 7:40, and Lenny left at 7:00. Benny took the No. 55 bus (4), so Denny took the No. 29 (1), Kenny the No. 42 and Lenny the No. 16.

Thus:

Benny - 7:40 - No. 55 - cinema;
Denny - 7:15 - No. 29 - theater;
Kenny - 7:30 - No. 42 - restaurant;
Lenny - 7:00 - No. 16 - nightclub.

66

No child found 13 or 16 eggs (grid). Danny found either 14 or 17 eggs (clue 1) and Edgar found 12 or 14 (clue 2). The child with the yellow basket found either 15 or 18 eggs (3) and isn't Gordon. Nor is he Ivan (1), so Henry's basket was yellow. The child with the purple basket found at least 15 eggs (2), so Henry found 18 eggs. The child with the scarlet basket thus found 17 eggs (3) and isn't Gordon, so Ivan. Thus Danny found 14 eggs and (1) the child with the brown basket found 12 eggs. By elimination, the child who found 15 eggs is Gordon and Edgar found 12 eggs. Gordon's basket was purple (2), so Danny's was green.

Thus:

Danny - green - 14 eggs;
Edgar - brown - 12 eggs;
Gordon - purple - 15 eggs;
Henry - yellow - 18 eggs;
Ivan - scarlet - 17 eggs.

67

Walter is married to Elizabeth (clue 3) and their child isn't Paul. Maria and Susan (the two girls) were born to either Barbara and her partner or Jerry and his partner (clue 2), so Walter's and Elizabeth's child is Daniel. Paul was born at 5:00 P.M. (3), so Barbara's daughter was born at 2:00 P.M. (2). Daniel was thus born at 11:00 A.M. (1), Gregory's child at 2:00 P.M. and Linda's at 8:00 A.M. Linda's child is thus a girl (2), so Rebecca is Paul's mother. Jerry's child was born at 8:00 A.M. (2), so Andrew's was born at 5:00 P.M. Susan's father isn't Gregory (1), so Jerry. Maria's father is Gregory.

Thus:

Andrew - Rebecca - Paul - 5:00 P.M.;
Gregory - Barbara - Maria - 2:00 P.M.;
Jerry - Linda - Susan - 8:00 A.M.;
Walter - Elizabeth - Daniel - 11:00 A.M.

68

The Armosians didn't visit island A at all, the Balerans didn't go to B, the Calieris didn't go to C, and the Daconians didn't go to D (intro). Thus the Calieris didn't go to B in April (clue 3), nor to D (farthest south) in April (clue 4), so to A. The Balerans didn't go to C in April (1), so D. The Balerans didn't go to C in July (3), so they went to A in July and C in October. By elimination, the Daconians were the merchants who visited A in October. The Daconians thus went to C

in April (2) and B in July. The Calieris went to D in July, so to B in October. The Armosians went to B in April, C in July, and D in October.

Thus (April - July - October):

Armosians - B - C - D;
Balerans - D - A - C;
Calieris - A - D - B;
Daconians - C - B - A.

69

Monday night's date wasn't Joanne's (clue 1), Sylvia's (clue 2), Pamela's, or Veronica's (3), so Kate's. Alan's date was on Tuesday (2) and Sylvia's was on Wednesday. Pamela's date was on Thursday (3) and Veronica's, on Friday, so Joanne's date was on Tuesday. Martin's date was on Monday (1), and Terry's was on Wednesday. Veronica's date wasn't with Carl (4), so Peter. Pamela dated Carl.

Thus:

Joanne - Alan - Tuesday;
Kate - Martin - Monday;
Pamela - Carl - Thursday;
Sylvia - Terry - Wednesday;
Veronica - Peter - Friday.

70

Three of the four gifts are the jigsaw, the one with a turquoise bow, and the one wrapped in blue paper (clue 3). Since Denise gave none of these (clue 3), she's the person who gave the embroidery set in purple paper with a yellow bow (4). The gift in white paper with an orange bow (1) is (by elimination) the jigsaw puzzle. The woman (1) who gave it is thus Roberta. Larry's present wasn't the book (2), so knitting items, and Michael gave the book. Since Larry's paper was pink (2), Michael's was blue. Michael's bow wasn't turquoise (3), so red, and Larry's was turquoise.

Thus (paper - bow):
Denise - embroidery set - purple - yellow;
Larry - knitting items - pink - turquoise;
Michael - book - blue - red;
Roberta - jigsaw puzzle - white - orange.

71

The Marita is older than Liam's car (clue 2) and older than Kirk's car (clue 3) but newer than the gray car. So the Marita is 4 years old, the gray car is 5 years old, and Liam's and Kirk's cars are either 2 and/or 3 years old. Melvyn bought the blue car (4), which is thus 4 years old (Marita, above), so Jack bought the gray car. Liam bought the Teant (2), so (4) the Arravo is 2 years old. The Teant is thus 3 years old. By elimination, Jack bought the Skorder and Kirk bought the Arravo. Liam's car is white (1) and Kirk's is green.

Thus:
Jack - Skorder - 5 years - gray;
Kirk - Arravo - 2 years - green;
Liam - Teant - 3 years - white;
Melvyn - Marita - 4 years - blue.

72

The two people not mentioned by name in clue 1 are Brian and Moira, who are thus the ones with either a martini or coffee. The person with lemonade is next to Brian (clue 2) and Claire is between Simon and Daniel (clue 1), so Claire isn't drinking lemonade. A man has mineral water (3), so Claire has beer. By elimination, the man in seat B with mineral water is either Daniel or Simon. If he's Daniel, then (1) Claire is in seat A, which (since she has beer, above) isn't possible (3). So Simon is in seat B, Claire in C (1), Daniel in D, the martini-drinker in E, and the coffee-drinker in A. By elimination, Daniel has lemonade, so Brian is in E (2) and Moira is in seat A.

Thus:
Seat A - Moira - coffee;
Seat B - Simon - mineral water;
Seat C - Claire - beer;
Seat D - Daniel - lemonade;
Seat E - Brian - martini.

73

The person who moved on Tuesday isn't Mr. Dean (clue 1), Mrs. Player or Ms. Byron (clue 2), so Mrs. Ford. Mrs. Ford's item cost either $150 or $200 (2), as did Mr. Dean's (1). The item that cost $300 didn't belong to Mrs. Player (2), so Ms. Byron. Thus Mrs. Player's item cost $250 and (2) was the lamp. The table thus didn't cost $200 to replace (3), so $150 and the vase costs $200. So Ms. Byron's item was the clock. It was broken on Wednesday (1) and Mr. Dean's item on Friday. So Mrs. Player's item was broken on Monday. The item that was broken on Tuesday (above) cost either $150 or $200 to replace, so not $100 more than Mr. Dean's item, which also cost either $150 or $200. Thus Monday's item cost $100 more to replace than Mr. Dean's (1). So Mr. Dean's was $150 (table) and the $200 vase belonged to Mrs. Ford.

Thus:

Ms. Byron - Wednesday - clock - $300;

Mr. Dean - Friday - table - $150;

Mrs. Ford - Tuesday - vase - $200;

Mrs. Player - Monday - lamp - $250.

74

Rachel is going to the Mediterranean and Theo to the Pacific Islands (clue 4). Dora and her husband Ronnie (clue 1) aren't going to South America or Australasia, so the Indian Ocean. Theo's wife isn't Thelma or Eileen (2), so Christine. Thelma isn't going to Australasia (3), so South America. Thus Eileen is going to Australasia. Her husband isn't Bill (2) or Peter (3), so Malcolm. Thelma's husband isn't Peter (3), so Bill. Peter's wife is Rachel.

Thus:

Bill - Thelma - South America;

Malcolm - Eileen - Australasia;

Peter - Rachel - Mediterranean;

Ronnie - Dora - Indian Ocean;

Theo - Christine - Pacific Islands.

75

The person who travels for 15 minutes isn't surnamed Johnson (clue 1), nor Raille (clue 2) (since no one travels for 18 minutes, grid). The manager is surnamed Miller and takes longer than 15 minutes (3), so Parry travels for 15 minutes. The Chief Teller isn't Johnson or Parry (1), so Raille who (2) travels for either 17 or 20 minutes. The one who travels for 23 minutes isn't surnamed Johnson (1), so Miller. Thus Johnson travels for 17 minutes (1) and Raille (Chief Teller, above) for 20 minutes. Charles travels for 23 minutes (2). The person surnamed Johnson (Mr., 1) is thus Jeremy, and Trina travels for 15 minutes, so Hazel travels for 20 minutes. Jeremy is the Assistant Manager (4), so Trina is the Secretary.

Thus:

Charles - Miller - Manager - 23 minutes;

Hazel - Raille - Chief Teller - 20 minutes;

Jeremy - Johnson - Asst. Manager - 17 minutes;

Trina - Parry - Secretary - 15 minutes.

76

The person who spent 6½ hours in the garden on Saturday isn't Gerda (clue 1), Bill (clue 2), Gina (3), or Brian (4), so Bert. Bert didn't work in the garden for 3 hours on Sunday (5). The person who spent 3 hours in the garden on Sunday isn't Gerda (1), Bill (2), or Brian (4), so Gina. Gina worked for 4 hours on Saturday (3). The person who worked in the garden for 3½ hours on Sunday isn't Gerda (1), Bill (2), or Brian (4), so Bert. The one who worked for 4½ hours on Sunday isn't Gerda (1) or Bill (2), so Brian. Brian worked in the garden for 4½ hours on Saturday (4). Bill worked in the garden for 6 hours on Sunday and 5 hours on Saturday (2), so Gerda worked 6 hours on Saturday and 5 hours on Sunday.

Thus (Saturday - Sunday):
Bert - 6½ hours - 3½ hours;
Bill - 5 hours - 6 hours;
Brian - 4½ hours - 4½ hours;
Gerda - 6 hours - 5 hours;
Gina - 4 hours - 3 hours.

77

Queen Charlotte's reign was 1816–24 (clue 1), so King David's reign was 1802–16 (clue 2). King Albert's reign was 1876–90 (14 years) (1). Queen Henrietta's reign was 1824–50 (1 and 3) and King Steven's was 1850–76. King Michael's reign was 1824–50 (4) and Queen Tabitha's was 1802–16.

By elimination, King Alfonso's was 1816–24. Queen Anne wasn't married to King Steven (3), so King Albert. Queen Margaret was married to King Steven.

Thus:
1802–16 - David - Tabitha;
1816–24 - Alfonso - Charlotte;
1824–50 - Michael - Henrietta;
1850–76 - Steven - Margaret;
1876–90 - Albert - Anne.

78

The man with 5 years' experience didn't climb Mt. McKinley (clue 1), Mt. Hood, or El Capitan (clue 2) or Mt. Foraker (3), so Mt. Rainier. Eric who climbed Mt. McKinley thus has 7 years' experience (1). The man with 6 years' experience didn't climb El Capitan (2) or Mt. Foraker (3), so Mt. Hood and (2) Frank has 5 years' experience. Thus Burt who climbed Mt. Foraker (3) has 10 years' experience and Dennis has 6 years'. By elimination, Alan climbed El Capitan and has 9 years' experience.

Thus:
Alan - 9 years' experience - El Capitan;
Burt - 10 years' experience - Mt. Foraker;
Dennis - 6 years' experience - Mt. Hood;
Eric - 7 years' experience - Mt. McKinley;
Frank - 5 years' experience - Mt. Rainier.

79

No one's pupils brought in 52 boxes (grid). Laura's pupils brought in 2 more boxes than Sarah's (clue 3), so Laura's didn't bring in 54 boxes. Thus the teacher whose pupils brought in 48 tubes isn't Laura (clue 4). So Laura's brought in 50 tubes (3) and Sarah's brought in 48 tubes and (4) 54 boxes. Laura's brought in 56 boxes (3). Since no teacher's pupils brought in 52 boxes, Roger's brought in 42 tubes (2) and the pupils of the teacher surnamed Barton brought in 48 boxes. The teacher surnamed Barton isn't Roger (2), so Pete. By elimination, Pete's pupils brought in 46 tubes and Roger's brought in 50 boxes. Since Pete's surname is Barton (48 boxes, above), Laura's is Hope (1) and Roger's is Smith. Sarah's surname is Lawson.

Thus:

Laura - Hope - 56 boxes - 50 tubes;
Pete - Barton - 48 boxes - 46 tubes;
Roger - Smith - 50 boxes - 42 tubes;
Sarah - Lawson - 54 boxes - 48 tubes.

80

Baggsia grows in the mountains (clue 1) and Aftonia in the swamp (clue 4). The desert plant has orange flowers (2). Torringtona has yellow flowers and isn't from the forest (3), so seashore. The forest plant isn't Laderia (3), so Storysia, and Laderia is from the desert. The scarlet-flowered plant isn't Baggsia or Aftonia (1), so Storysia. Aftonia's flowers aren't pink (4), so purple. Baggsia has pink flowers.

Thus:

Aftonia - purple - swamp;
Baggsia - pink - mountain;
Laderia - orange - desert;
Storysia - scarlet - forest;
Torringtona - yellow - seashore.

81

Car C didn't have a dent (clue 3), so Alice's car with a dent (clue 1) is B. Car A (farthest left) isn't the convertible (4), so (1) the coupé. C is the pickup (3), so the convertible is D (1) and B is the sedan. Roger's isn't A (2), so C (4), and D is the convertible, which (2) needs a repair to its headlights. C hasn't a rust hole (3), so the trunk lock needs work. Stephanie's isn't D (5), so A. Thomas owns car D. Stephanie's has a rust hole.

Thus:

Car A - coupé - rust hole - Stephanie;
Car B - sedan - dent - Alice;
Car C - pickup - trunk lock - Roger;
Car D - convertible - headlights - Thomas.

82

The picture with 6 (most) flowers wasn't painted by Florence (clue 2), so by Elizabeth (clue 3). Florence's hasn't 5 flowers (2), so Graham's has 5 (3). Elizabeth's picture hasn't 5 or 6 birds (1), so 3 (4), and David's has

SOLUTIONS

2. Elizabeth's has 5 trees (1), so Florence's has 4 trees and 2 flowers (2). David's has 4 flowers. David's has 3 trees (4) and Graham's has 2. Graham's picture hasn't 6 birds (5), so 5, and Florence's has 6 birds.

Thus (birds - trees - flowers):
David - 2 - 3 - 4;
Elizabeth - 3 - 5 - 6;
Florence - 6 - 4 - 2;
Graham - 5 - 2 - 5.

83

Remember throughout that each jar and lid are in two different colors (intro). Jar D (farthest right) isn't blue (clue 1), violet or red (clue 2), so green. Either A is violet and B is red (2), or B is violet and C is red. In other words, jar B is either red or violet. The blue jar isn't A (1), so it's C. Thus A is violet (2) and B is red. Jar A's lid isn't blue (1) or red (2), so green. Jar D has a blue lid (1) and B contains parsley. By elimination, B has a violet lid and C has a red lid. C contains thyme (2). Jar D doesn't contain sage (3), so rosemary. The sage is in jar A.

Thus (herb - jar - lid):
Jar A - sage - violet - green;
Jar B - parsley - red - violet;
Jar C - thyme - blue - red;
Jar D - rosemary - green - blue.

84

The sum of $1,200 (least) wasn't raised for St. John's (clue 1), St. Mary's (clue 2) or St. Paul's (3), so St. Andrew's. The event at St. Paul's was a church sale (3). Since it raised more than $1,200 (2), the sports day wasn't held to raise funds for St. Andrew's. Nor was it for St. Mary's (2), so St. John's. It wasn't organized by Reverends Frazer or Glade (1), or Stone (2), so White. It didn't raise $2,700 (3), so (1) Reverend Frazer raised $1,700 and Reverend White raised $2,200. The amount raised for St. Mary's (2) was $1,700 (Reverend Frazer, above), so the dance was at St. Andrew's (1) and the auction at St. Mary's. By elimination the event at St. Paul's raised $2,700, thus the priest at St. Paul's isn't Reverend Stone (2), so Reverend Glade. Reverend Stone is the priest at St. Andrew's.

Thus:
St. Andrew's - Rev. Stone - dance - $1,200;
St. John's - Rev. White - sports day - $2,200;
St. Mary's - Rev. Frazer - auction - $1,700;
St. Paul's - Rev. Glade - church sale - $2,700.

85

Jill's surname is Potter (clue 3), so the person surnamed Richardson is Keith (clue 2). Ian's surname isn't Thorne (1), so Stockton, and Hope's surname is Thorne. Hope isn't at consoles A or D (2), so the contestant from Eastwood is at C (1); Ian, at D, and Hope, at B. Keith from Southville (2) is at A, so Jill is at C. The West Hill contestant is at D (3), so the contestant at console B is from North Bay.

Thus:

Console A - Keith - Richardson
- Southville;

Console B - Hope - Thorne -
North Bay;

Console C - Jill - Potter - Eastwood;

Console D - Ian - Stockton - West Hill.

86

Ned's cat is called Lucky (clue 4). Caesar lives at either No. 2 or No. 3 (clue 1) and Naomi, at either No. 1 or No. 4 (2), so Caesar isn't Naomi's cat. Caesar doesn't belong to Nigel or Norman (1), so Nancy. Thus Nancy is at No. 3 (3), Nigel at No. 2 (1), and Norman at No. 5. Ned isn't at No. 4 (4), so No. 1. Naomi is at No. 4. Duke lives at No. 5 (2) and Sam at No. 2 (3). Felix lives at No. 4.

Thus:

No. 1 - Lucky - Ned;

No. 2 - Sam - Nigel;

No. 3 - Caesar - Nancy;

No. 4 - Felix - Naomi;

No. 5 - Duke - Norman.

87

The woman whose favorite is slalom had the 10-day vacation (clue 4), so the woman whose favorite is Langlauf had the 14-day vacation (clue 3). Vicky, who prefers to snowboard (1), thus had the 9-day vacation and Teri's was for 7 days. Tessa's was thus for 10 days (3), so Lavinia's was for 14 days. By elimination, the ski jump is Teri's favorite, thus she went to Whistler (2). Vicky went to Kicking Horse (3). Tessa (10 days, above) didn't go to Mount Cain (4), so Lake Louise. Lavinia went to Mount Cain.

Thus:

Lavinia - Mount Cain - 14 days
- Langlauf;

Teri - Whistler - 7 days - ski jump;

Tessa - Lake Louise - 10 days
- slalom;

Vicky - Kicking Horse - 9 days
- snowboard.

88

Debra took 12 bags (clue 4). The woman who took 21 bags isn't Pamela (clue 2) or Amanda (3), so Martha. Pamela takes paper (2). Martha doesn't take aluminum (1) or glass (3), so plastic. Debra doesn't take glass (4), so aluminum. Amanda takes glass. Debra (12 bags) didn't go on Tuesday (2) and Martha (21 bags) didn't go on Thursday (3), so (1) Debra went on Monday and Martha on Tuesday. Pamela took 18 bags (2) so Amanda took 15. She went on

Wednesday (4), so Pamela went on Thursday.

Thus:

Amanda - glass - Wednesday - 15 bags;

Debra - aluminum - Monday - 12 bags;

Martha - plastic - Tuesday - 21 bags;

Pamela - paper - Thursday - 18 bags.

89

No one moved in on Friday (grid). Dean moved in on either Tuesday or Wednesday (clue 1), as did Ian and his wife, Thelma (clue 2). Sandra's husband isn't Dean (1), so she moved in on Thursday, Dean, on Wednesday, and Mr. & Mrs. Hopwood on Saturday. Ian and Thelma moved in on Tuesday (2), Mr. & Mrs. Jarvis, on Wednesday and Mr. & Mrs. Norton, on Thursday. By elimination, Ian and Thelma are Mr. & Mrs. Pringle. Hannah's surname isn't Jarvis (3), so Alice's is Jarvis and Hannah's is Hopwood. Hannah's husband isn't Richard (4), so Mike. Richard is married to Sandra.

Thus:

Dean - Alice - Jarvis - Wednesday;

Ian - Thelma - Pringle - Tuesday;

Mike - Hannah - Hopwood - Saturday;

Richard - Sandra - Norton - Thursday.

90

Steven won 4 games in the second set (clue 1), so Thelma won 3 in the second (clue 4) and 6 in the first. Peter won 3 in the first (1). The person who won 4 in the first isn't Steven (2) or Veronica (3), so Jane. The winner of 6 in the second isn't Veronica (2) or Peter (3), so Jane. Thus Jane's total was 10, so (5) Peter won 7 in the second. Veronica won 7 in the first set (3), so Steven won 5 in the first and (2) Veronica won 5 in the second set.

Thus (first set - second set):

Jane - 4 - 6;

Peter - 3 - 7;

Steven - 5 - 4;

Thelma - 6 - 3;

Veronica - 7 - 5.

91

No pill was taken at 10:30 (grid). The 7:30 drink was apple juice (clue 2), so the brown pill was taken at 9:30 (clue 3), water was drunk at 8:30 and the red pill was taken at 11:30. The vitamin K pill was taken with milk (1), so the 11:30 drink was coffee and the vitamin A pill was taken at 7:30. The vitamin K pill was brown (3). The blue pill wasn't taken at 7:30 (2), so 8:30. The 7:30 pill was white. The vitamin C pill wasn't blue (2), so red. The vitamin E pill was blue.

Thus:

7:30 A.M. - white - vitamin A - apple juice;
8:30 A.M. - blue - vitamin E - water;
9:30 A.M. - brown - vitamin K - milk;
11:30 A.M. - red - vitamin C - coffee.

92

Remember throughout that the name of each girl and the two colors in which she is dressing her doll begin with three different letters of the alphabet (intro). Gloria's doll thus hasn't a blue jacket (clue 1) and Briony's hasn't a green dress. The doll with a red dress and blue jacket (clue 3) doesn't belong to Polly, so (by elimination) to Tina. Polly's doll has a red jacket (2). The doll with a blue dress and pink jacket (4) isn't Rosemary's, so Gloria's. Briony's doll will wear a pink dress (1), but not a turquoise jacket (5), so a green jacket. The turquoise jacket will thus be worn with the green dress. Polly's doll will wear a red jacket (above), so a turquoise dress. Rosemary's doll will wear a green dress.

Thus (dress - jacket):

Briony - pink - green;
Gloria - blue - pink;
Polly - turquoise - red;
Rosemary - green - turquoise;
Tina - red - blue.

93

The table was bought in the 3rd store where they weren't served by Jennifer (clue 3), so they bought the oven in Arkwright's (clue 1), which was visited 2nd, and Jennifer assisted in the 1st store. Wise Buys was visited 3rd (2) and Home Help, where the assistant is Michael, was visited 4th. Thus Capital K was visited 1st. William doesn't work in Wise Buys (3), so Nancy works in Wise Buys and William in Arkwright's. The drapes weren't purchased from Capital K (4), so Home Help. The teapot was bought in Capital K.

Thus:

Arkwright's - second - William - oven;
Capital K - first - Jennifer - teapot;
Home Help - fourth - Michael - drapes;
Wise Buys - third - Nancy - table.

94

Butch is the lead guitarist (clue 2) and Shiner is the singer (clue 3). Animal isn't the bass guitarist (1), so he's the drummer and Wild Man is the bass guitarist. Charles is Wild Man (3). The man who has been with the band for 6 months isn't Animal (1), Butch (2), or Shiner (3), so Wild Man. Edward has thus been with the band for 7 months and Animal for 9 months (1), so Shiner for 8 months. Animal isn't William (2), so Arthur. Butch has been with the band for 7 months (2) and William for 8 months.

Thus:

Animal - Arthur - drummer -
   9 months;

Butch - Edward - lead guitarist -
   7 months;

Shiner - William - singer - 8 months;

Wild Man - Charles - bass guitarist -
   6 months.

95

The woman born on the 10th isn't Jane (clue 1), Judy (clue 3), or Jenny (4), so Joanne. Joanne isn't the woman whose birthday is six days earlier in its month than Jane's (1), so Jane was born on the 22nd and Joanne is two years older than the woman born on the 16th. Thus Jenny is either 23 or 24 (4), Joanne is 22, and (1) the woman born on the 16th is 20. By elimination, Judy is 20. Jane (22nd, above) isn't 23 (2), so she's 24 and Jenny is 23. Jenny was born on the 13th. Judy's birthday is in August (3), so Jenny's is in October (2) and Jane's in June. Joanne's birthday is in April.

Thus:

Jane - 24 - 22nd - June;

Jenny - 23 - 13th - October;

Joanne - 22 - 10th - April;

Judy - 20 - 16th - August.

96

Remember throughout that each woman is wearing three different colors (intro). The one in the blue coat has an apricot scarf (clue 3), thus not an apricot hat. The woman in the apricot coat has neither an apricot or blue hat nor an apricot or blue scarf (intro and clue 1), so the woman in the apricot coat is wearing either a lime or pink hat, as is the woman in the blue coat, and neither has a blue scarf. Lynne has a pink hat, but not a lime scarf (2), so her scarf is either apricot or blue. Thus her coat isn't apricot, so (above) Lynne's coat is blue. Her scarf is apricot and (3) Martine's is pink. By elimination, the woman in the apricot coat has a lime hat, so her scarf is pink. Paula's scarf isn't blue (4), so lime; thus her coat is pink, and Olga has a lime coat and blue scarf. Olga's hat thus isn't blue, so apricot. Paula's hat is blue.

Thus (coat - hat - scarf):

Lynne - blue - pink - apricot;

Martine - apricot - lime - pink;

Olga - lime - apricot - blue;

Paula - pink - blue - lime.

97

Remember throughout that each "new" picture is made of three "old" pictures (intro). Superman's head is with Buck Rogers's body (clue 1) and Iceman's head has Spider-Man's body (clue 3). Batman's body isn't with Buck Rogers's head (2), so Spider-Man's. Batman's head isn't with Superman's body (4), so Iceman's body. Superman's body is thus with Buck Rogers's head. Spider-Man's legs are with Batman's head (4). Superman's head and Buck Rogers's body aren't with Batman's legs (1), so Iceman's. Spider-Man's head and Batman's body aren't with Buck Rogers's legs (2), so Superman's. By elimination, Buck Rogers's legs are with Iceman's head, Buck Rogers's head is with Batman's legs, and Spider-Man's head is with Superman's legs.

Thus (head - body - legs):
Batman - Iceman - Spider-Man;
Buck Rogers - Superman - Batman;
Iceman - Spider-Man - Buck Rogers;
Spider-Man - Batman - Superman;
Superman - Buck Rogers - Iceman.

98
Remember throughout that in every case, each person paid one premium in any one month (intro) and no one paid car insurance in October, health insurance in November, or home insurance in September (grid). The person who paid for home insurance in November and car insurance in December (clue 3) isn't Cheryl or Sophie (clue 1) or Graham (2), so James. So James's health insurance and Sophie's home insurance were paid in October (1), and Cheryl paid her car insurance in September. Graham paid his health insurance in September (2), his home insurance in December and his car insurance in

August. By elimination, Cheryl paid her home insurance in August, so her health insurance in December. Sophie paid her health insurance in August and her car insurance in November.

Thus (car - health - home):
Cheryl - September - December - August;
Graham - August - September - December;
James - December - October - November;
Sophie - November - August - October.

99
The surname of the child who made 14 (most) mistakes isn't Carter (clue 1), Adams (clue 2), Willard, or Evans (3), so Robertson, who (2) is Jim. The one who made 12 mistakes isn't surnamed Carter (1) or Adams (2), so Evans, and Willard made 11 mistakes. Cora made either 11 or 12 mistakes (1), so her surname is either Evans or Willard (above). The Adams child and Carter child made 8 and/or 9 mistakes. The Adams child isn't Sally or Larry (2), so Brian. Thus Larry is the boy surnamed Carter (1). Larry made 8 mistakes (4) and Brian 9. Cora made 11 (1), so Sally made 12 mistakes.

Thus:
Brian - Adams - 9 mistakes;
Cora - Willard - 11 mistakes;
Jim - Robertson - 14 mistakes;
Larry - Carter - 8 mistakes;
Sally - Evans - 12 mistakes.

100

The girl who lives at No. 1 isn't 11 years old (clue 3), so (clue 4) she's 12 and Sue Ireland is 10. The surname of the girl who lives at No. 4 isn't Goodman (2), Harper (3), or Forbes (5), so Ireland (Sue, above). Rosie thus lives at No. 2 (2). Maggie doesn't live at No. 3 (1), so No. 1. Ellen thus lives at No. 3. Since Maggie is 12 (above), Ellen is 11 (1). By elimination, Rosie is 9 years old. Maggie's surname is Forbes (5). Rosie's surname isn't Goodman (2), so Harper. Ellen is Miss Goodman.

Thus:

Ellen - Goodman - No. 3 - 11;
Maggie - Forbes - No. 1 - 12;
Rosie - Harper - No. 2 - 9;
Sue - Ireland - No. 4 - 10.